LIFTING UP HOPE, LIVING OUT JUSTICE

METHODIST WOMEN AND THE SOCIAL GOSPEL

Alice G. Knotts

Lifting Up Hope, Living Out Justice

Methodist Women And The Social Gospel

Alice G. Knotts

619-955-0925
frontrowliving@yahoo.com
www.progressivechristianbookstore.com

ISBN: 978-0-9794194-0-9

Book and cover design by Brenda Riddell

To my parents,

J. Ross Knotts and Marjorie Cooley Knotts

and my grandson,

Andrew Joseph Bowman.

"She's a whole cathedral."

Miss Winifred Chappell

Winifred Chappell, 1912 or 1913.

CONTENTS

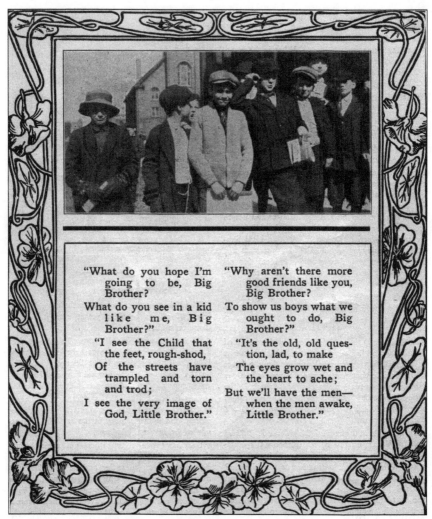

"What do you hope I'm
    going to be, Big
    Brother?

What do you see in a kid
    like me, Big
    Brother?"

"I see the Child that
    the feet, rough-shod,

Of the streets have
    trampled and torn
    and trod;

I see the very image of
    God, Little Brother."

"Why aren't there more
    good friends like you,
    Big Brother?

To show us boys what we
    ought to do, Big
    Brother?"

"It's the old, old ques-
    tion, lad, to make

The eyes grow wet and
    the heart to ache;

But we'll have the men—
    when the men awake,
    Little Brother."

A woman with boys from Chicago, 1914.

~

Acknowledgments

Many friends and colleagues have helped to bring this book together. I especially appreciate the help of Dr. Jeanne Miller Schmidt, Betsy Cooper, The Rev. Dr. Beth Cooper, Dr. Carolyn DeSwarte Gifford, Dr. Rima Schultz, The Rev. Kathryn Johnson, Dr. Virginia Lapham, The Rev. Dr. George McClain, The Rev. Dr. Joanne Carlson Brown, The Rev. Ross and Marge Knotts, Joe Knotts, Eva Nalhi, Ulrike Guthrie, John Coffey, Brenda Riddell, Barbara Campbell, and Becky Louter. Thank you, everyone!

Cover photo: Ellen Gates Starr holding a boy. They sit looking at Hull House, not pictured. Photo provided courtesy of the Jane Addams Memorial Collection, Special Collections Department, Richard J. Daley Library, University of Illinois, Chicago. Used with permission.

Most pictures are from Hilda S. Steele's 1909 memory book from Chicago Training School Archives collection of albums, Bertha Fowler, Box 5, United Library of Garrett-Evangelical Theological Seminary and Seabury-Western Theological Seminary, Evanston, Illinois, and used with permission.

Thanks to the University of Chicago Library for a copy of the photo of Mary McDowell from the cover of *The Commons: A Monthly Record Devoted to Aspects of Life and Labor from the Social Settlement Point of View*, Chicago, Vol. II, No. 9, January 1898.

The Divine Right of Childhood

It is the divine right of childhood to be mothered, and no institution, however perfect, can stand in the place of a real mother. "Our superintendent" may see that we are properly clothed and fed, but "my mother" kisses the bumps and bruises.

Deaconess with children in the snow, 1914.

~

INTRODUCTION

LIVING AND BREATHING THE WHOLE GOSPEL

THIS BOOK IS about five women whose Christian thinking and faith inspire us to reach higher, dig deeper, and go farther than we dreamed possible toward making this world a better place. These women aspired to serve others with a love as broad as God's love. They aimed to make Earth a little more heavenly. By recognizing their identity as children of God and their paramount calling to serve God by helping others, they surmounted amazing obstacles in order to bring a sense of human dignity, respect, and justice to the world around them.

Mary McDowell, Isabelle Horton, Bertha Fowler, Grace Scribner, and Winifred Chappell concluded that good intentions, a good heart, and positive actions are not enough to create a better world: it takes organizing, networking, and political action. A faith focused only on personal conversion, faith formation, and a life of worship is not complete. For them, responding to the *whole* gospel meant engaging evil as it was manifest in social problems and providing help, hope, and respect for all persons regardless of their station in life.

One cannot tell the stories of these women without also telling the stories of three movements: the settlement movement, the deaconess movement, and the social gospel movement. Each played a major role in shaping society at the turn of the last century. The five women we meet in this book both helped to shape, and were shaped by, these movements.

Finally, this book is about an organization which celebrates the 100th anniversary of its founding this year. The Methodist Federation for Social Service (now, the Methodist Federation for Social Action) was founded to promote understanding and acceptance of the whole gospel. The Methodist Federation interpreted this to mean that Christians should participate in a compassionate justice-seeking approach to social problems.

The stories of MacDowell, Horton, Fowler, Scribner and Chappell, all of whom lived a hundred years ago, are remarkably pertinent today. Between 1907 and 1914, these five women developed cutting edge social gospel thinking about the inter-relationships of social problems. They learned from first hand experiences that charity and minor social reforms would not solve the problem of massive poverty and human misery in the U.S. These women called for a change in national priorities. They declared that the nation's most important resource was its people. They saw that a nation bent on capitalist expansion paid scant attention to the value of human life, meaning, fulfillment, and well-being.

Likewise, the principles upon which the Methodist Federation for Social Service was founded are as relevant today as they were in 1907. The Methodist Federation set out to change the way people looked at the world. The Federation lobbied for federal regulation of foods and drugs. At great financial cost and loss of life to workers, labor unions wrested from industry the right of workers to have one day a week of rest, a limit of 12 hours of work in one day, child labor laws, and the right of workers to organize. The Methodist Federation helped the unions win public support for these changes.

The writing and leadership of the five women in this book influenced MFSS, which, in turn, had national impact in shaping American life. The Federation benefited greatly from the contributions of these women. For all of them, MFSS provided a platform for their knowledge, wisdom and insights to be shared.

What does it take for people to become such remarkable witnesses to their faith? The people in these stories who were exemplary, forward thinking, and courageous went through a process to get there. They dedicated themselves to following their faith commitment with passion and to developing the skills needed in their situation. Each of these women left behind other possibilities for her life in order to obtain higher education. Each was motivated by her Christian faith. Each made a life commitment to use her professional abilities to work for a better world. In a culture where women typically did not combine a career with marriage, these women chose not to have husbands or children, but devoted their full attention to living out their call to Christian faith.

These early Methodist women came from homes and Christian backgrounds in which they learned the importance of doing what is good. Through their involvement in the social gospel movement and the deaconess movement and their education and exposure to massive human problems, they came to see that they could made a difference by undertaking small tasks that were part of larger tasks that could in turn affect big issues.

These Methodist women found the nurture and support they needed to stand up for poor people against injustices of the social system. That nurture came from inner courage fed by the belief that fulfillment of basic human needs is more important than having things or property.

Rarely do people who benefit from a social system become the leaders who raise the moral conscience of the nation. The women in these stories typically were not women of means; they were simply women who were troubled by what they saw and experienced. Their lessons came from first-hand acquaintance with poverty, prejudice, deprivation, risk, and loss—experiences that helped them see inequities and envision a better society.

I came to the Methodist Federation in 1975, inspired by these five women's journeys and writings, and believing that if we tune our lives to God and set our lives on a path to make a difference in our society, we will be able to see progress. At this time of writing, society in the United States suffers from problems very similar to those of the past. The names and situations have changed, but many of the underlying human problems still exist. It is with dismay that I see ways this nation has reversed its priorities and moved backwards, disengaging from its moral responsibility to care for its residents and citizens. This could mean that we are stuck, but I don't think so. Perhaps knowing the history in these pages will inspire people to rise up once again to organize and engage not simply a personal gospel, but a social gospel, and signal an end to a social system based on sexism, heterosexism, economic class, and racism.

I pray that you will be inspired by these stories to be reminded what a difference people of faith can make when they band together. I hope that you will have the eyes of faith to see beyond past history and current evils that are wreaking havoc. May you have the patience and faith to know that your small action for good will have a ripple affect that can bless the world. I encourage you to join a group where you will have support from like-minded people who are open minded, compassionate, and willing to become involved in response to God's love for the whole world.

STUDY QUESTIONS

1. Who has inspired you to "reach higher, dig deeper, and go farther toward making this world a better place?" What spiritual grounding or faith commitments guide this person? What are some of the experiences that formed this person's commitment?
2. What has been your motivation when you have made choices that give back to the world and help others?
3. What do you think the author means by the phrase "the whole gospel?" When have you experienced it?

Sewing class at an institutional church, 1914

THE SOCIAL GOSPEL EMBRACES LIFE'S CONTEXT

B Y THE LATE 1800s in the U.S., the westward expansion for farm-land and gold had slowed. Americans were migrating to the cit-ies where jobs were available in the growing textile and garment industries, steel and railroading, meatpacking and manufacturing, cigar factories and shoemaking.

The single-owner business rapidly was being displaced. Corporate managers analyzed jobs scientifically and reduced them to simple component motions of mass production. Corporations developed anti-union policies to maintain long work hours and low wages. The corporations did not have or adhere to safety standards. Workers were locked into buildings and this practice sometimes led to terrible loss of life in fires. Small children worked the same long hours as their parents, los-ing fingers, limbs, or health in mines and factories. Rooms were not adequately lighted. Workers did not have suitable chairs or working conditions, nor did they receive anything approaching fair pay for the hours they toiled in such circumstances. In the industrial cities such as Boston, Chicago, Detroit and New York, the consequences of poverty created horrible conditions such as extensive child labor, lack of edu-cation, crowding, disease, high mortality rates, hunger, cold, lack of recreation, prostitution, gambling, drunkenness, child abuse, and wife battering. Many Americans were desperately poor while a few became very rich.

The rise of the social gospel movement between 1870 and 1890 came in response to unacceptable social conditions. Mentors, teachers, and theologians paved the way for social gospel thinking. Walter Rauschenbusch, considered the leading theologian of the social gospel movement, lived for a time in Rochester, New York, the home of leaders of the abolitionist movement. From 1886-97, he served as pastor of a German Baptist congregation in New York City in the Hell's Kitchen area, near Columbus Circle. The name Hell's Kitchen came from the crowded and unsanitary living conditions in city tenements. About 700,000 immigrants arrived in New York City each year.[1]

Rauschenbusch organized some friends into a group called the Brotherhood of the Kingdom. They rejected the notion that some people are born destined to be rich and others poor. They searched the Bible and concluded that the gospel that Jesus proclaimed was founded on the abolition of social inequality.[2] Jesus essentially called for a social revolution to treat all persons as equals. This was not merely a gospel of personal salvation. It engaged the attitudes of communities and societies. As an outgrowth of these discussions Rauschenbusch became an advocate of mandatory safety standards for industry, employee insurance compensation (worker's compensation), minimum wages, maximum work hours legislation, and improved housing standards.[3]

Some of the early Methodist social gospel leaders were influenced by another mentor, Borden Parker Bowne, who had studied under the German theologian Rudolph Hermann Loetze. As the leading professor of philosophy at Boston School of Theology from 1876-1910, Bowne influenced several generations of ministers.[4] George Albert Coe at the University of Chicago trained pastors and influenced deaconesses. Other Methodist social gospel leaders were shaped by their own experiences.

Baptists, Presbyterians, and British Methodists all organized unofficial church organizations to promote understanding and acceptance of the social gospel. Americans from the Methodist Episcopal Church

---

1. Maldwyn Allen Jones, *American Immigration* (Chicago: University of Chicago Press, c. 1960) 195.

2. Ronald C. White, Jr. and C. Howard Hopkins, *The Social Gospel: Religion and Reform in Changing America* (Philadelphia: Temple University Press, c. 1976) 40.

3. Glenn C. Altschuler, "Walter Rauschenbusch's Theology: The Church and the Social Gospel," *Foundations*, April-June, 1979, 40.

4. William McGuire King, "The Emergence of Social Gospel Radicalism in American Methodism," (Cambridge, Massachusetts: Harvard University, 1977) unpublished dissertation, 93, 94, 96, 97.

followed in 1907 with the Methodist Federation. Traditional histories of the Methodist Federation for Social Service describe the leadership of five key men. These men gathered ideas from Europe from the Wesleyan Methodist Union for Social Service and from Oxford University, where the founder of Methodism, John Wesley, had studied and worked.

Methodists have had a long heritage of commitment to social concerns. They believed that God's love for all people meant that people needed to assume social as well as personal responsibility for life. The core of their teaching was to love God and love their neighbor as they loved themselves.

Wesley preached Jesus' love for the poor. He left church buildings behind when he went outdoors to preach at 4 a.m. to miners on their way to work. He started schools, an orphanage, a free clinic, and small group support systems. He put into print cheap books and inexpensive health resources to help families. Methodists hesitantly used women as leaders in class meetings and small Christian fellowships. They opposed slavery and the rum and slave trade triangle. Within a few generations, British Methodists lifted a class of poor people out of poverty, teaching them to work hard, save money, and not spend it on smoking and drinking. Educated children moved up the economic ladder. To a surprising extent, Methodists did this in the U.S. in the early 1800s, but by the late 1800s, industrialization and urbanization overpowered what a church could do.

By the 1880s, the role of Methodist women in the church had expanded significantly with the development of three new avenues of service—the Woman's Home Missionary Society, the deaconess movement, and the settlement movement—that began to bring together women who shared the social gospel view that the liberation and salvation Jesus brought applied not only to individuals but also to social contexts.

Scattered local women's groups started and supported missionary projects, in 1880 forming the Woman's Home Missionary Society of the Methodist Episcopal Church (WHMS). The WHMS gathered offerings from these women's groups in order to provide things such as parsonages for pioneer clergy, orphanages for children, mission schools, and clinics.

The second new avenue of service, the deaconess movement in

the U.S., began in 1885 when Lucy Rider Meyer founded the Chicago Training School to prepare women for service to the church. The women whose stories are told in this book served as social workers and deaconesses in the Methodist Episcopal Church.

Deaconesses were women who gave their lives to serving people in need. As did the early Christians described in the Bible in the book of Acts, they held office in the church as people who serve. They were not ordained as ministers are, but were consecrated by the denomination and found their own position of employment in which they could be of Christian service. Deaconesses lived on meager salaries, usually in a house shared with other deaconesses that was appropriately enough called a Deaconess Home. In times of illness, they received care in public hospitals started by deaconesses and in old age lived in deaconess retirement homes. Deaconesses pre-dated social workers. To meet the physical and spiritual needs of people marginalized by society, they worked with migrants and immigrants in inner cities, persons facing discrimination, and especially women and children. Deaconesses are still at work. Today about 138 United Methodist deaconesses perform services to make Jesus Christ known. Their four point mission is to alleviate suffering, eradicate causes of injustice, facilitate the development of full human potential, and build global community through the church. Deaconesses still look for opportunities to be in cutting edge ministries, joining "the struggle to bring healing and to overcome injustices, choosing to go where others may not want to go."[5]

Lucy Rider Meyer envisioned that deaconesses could create a home in Chicago's crowded immigrant ward which would be a safe, warm, loving, caring place like a little bit of heaven on Earth. By 1888, the

---

5. *The Book of Discipline of The United Methodist Church 2004*, Para. 1313.2. "Theology of Mission and Relationship within the Church Office of Deaconess," 2007. Becky Louter, Deaconess, Deaconesses and Home Missioners, General Board of Global Ministries of The United Methodist Church. Nowadays deaconesses are paid wages, choose their own job and find their own housing. Today deaconess programs are growing again. Deaconesses started projects that serviced the needs of immigrants, poor people, the sick, women and children. Although many of the schools, homes, and hospitals started by deaconesses closed over the years, others evolved with name changes. Some still operate with "Deaconess" or "Methodist" as part of their name. Each of these projects was supported both by a national organization of women (the Woman's Home Missionary Society), by members of the community, and by local churches. From 1940-68, the deaconess program was part of the Woman's Division of the Board of Missions of The Methodist Church. Today a deaconess program is part of the General Board of Global Ministries of The United Methodist Church.

General Conference of the Methodist Episcopal Church gave official recognition to graduates of the school and members of the first class of graduates were consecrated as deaconesses.

From 1888 to 1904, the Chicago Training School sent out over a thousand deaconesses, harnessing and unleashing the power of women whose public roles and opportunities had up until then been curtailed by social limitations about what constituted appropriate roles for women. Graduates became founders, superintendents, and directors of many deaconess homes, girls' homes, schools, rest homes, hospitals, orphanages, and nursing homes. Without a doubt, thousands of men, women, and children experienced first hand benefits that were due to the dedication of these deaconesses and the hundreds of thousands of Methodist women who supported them.

The third new avenue of service was the settlement movement. This movement started and ran community centers in urban ghettos that were dealing with immigrants and others who were stuck in poverty, and living in slum conditions. The settlement movement came to the U.S. from Edinburgh, Scotland,[6] and expanded to Chicago with Hull House, started by Jane Addams in 1889, and Northwestern University Settlement launched by Northwestern in 1891. In 1894, the Christian Union and philanthropic committee of the University of Chicago founded the University of Chicago Settlement in Packingtown. That's where Mary McDowell worked.[7] These latter two settlements had a formative influence on Harry Ward who was to serve for 36 years as the executive secretary (director) of the Methodist Federation for Social Service.

The deaconess movement, the settlement movement, the social gospel movement and the Methodist Federation for Social Service all touched the lives of Mary McDowell, Isabelle Horton, Bertha Fowler, Grace Scribner, and Winifred Chappell. This group of women initially was located in Chicago, an important center for the network of principal contributors to the Methodist social gospel movement.

The central figures in this story brought together a broader network of people of faith who were working with deaconess programs, with social

---

6. Eugene P. Link, *Labor-Religion Prophet: The Times and Life of Harry F. Ward* (Boulder, CO: Westview Press, c. 1984) 17.

7. John Palmer Gavit, ed., *Bibliography of College, Social and University Settlements*, (Cambridge: Cooperative Press, 1897) Third edition, 20. Published for the College Settlements Association.

settlements, and with the Methodist Federation. Jane Addams was one person who helped weave patterns of cooperation between social settlements and deaconesses. In 1887, she lectured to students at the Chicago Training School, bringing fresh ideas from her recent tour of Europe.

This story is about a neighborhood network, the personal interconnections and proximity of leaders. In 1889, Addams founded Hull House on south Halsted Street, very close to the Chicago Training School on Dearborn Street. Hull House was also near Halsted Street Institutional Church where Isabelle (Belle) Horton, a Methodist deaconess, later served on staff. In 1898, Harry Ward served as head resident of Northwestern Settlement House, and became a professional colleague to Mary McDowell. In 1904, Ward was appointed pastor of Union Avenue Methodist Church, located just one block from the University of Chicago Settlement House.

Lucy Rider Meyer was influential as a teacher and mentor in the lives of Isabelle Horton and Bertha Fowler, two deaconesses who graduated from the Chicago Training School. Horton and Fowler, along with Mary McDowell, were active in the Methodist Federation for Social Service from the beginning. A few years later Grace Scribner and Winifred Chappell, also deaconesses and graduates of the Chicago Training School, became members of the Methodist Federation.

The years preceding the formation of the Methodist Federation were the incubator for radical social gospel thought. With immigration, urbanization, and industrialization, it felt as if the whole world had come to Chicago. The deaconesses brought to their work the power of God's love and the power of personal faith. The experiences of Methodist women in the heart of Packingtown and Chicago slums combined with the discrimination that they experienced as women to change their thinking. Dire poverty was wasting the health, lives, and opportunities of immigrants who had fled other nations because their own governments would not or could not give them political protection, food, work, or shelter. Women such as Mary McDowell encountered the widespread power of social evil—but also the social gospel's ability to embrace the totality of such evil and bend it toward justice.

STUDY QUESTIONS

1. "Jesus essentially called for a social revolution to treat all persons as equals." Do you agree or disagree? Where have you seen or experienced this? What did it feel like?
2. Read Matthew 5:1-12. Jesus talks about new personal and social attitudes that could make a difference in society. What is the main teaching of Jesus in this text?
3. What reasons does the author give to explain why Methodist women became involved in the social gospel movement?
4. Who does the kinds of things that the deaconesses did one hundred years ago?
5. Sometimes a crisis opens a new opportunity. What crisis faced the nation?

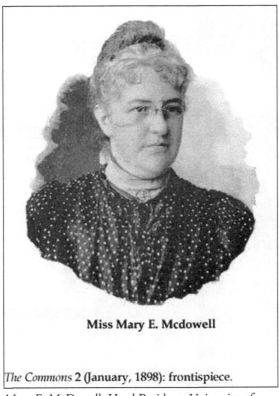

Miss Mary E. Mcdowell

The Commons 2 (January, 1898): frontispiece.

Mary E. McDowell, Head Resident, University of Chicago Settlement, Chicago, 1898. University of Chicago Library.

Deaconess with a boy, 1909.

Deaconess with a girl, 1909.

Deaconess with girls in front of I. Berger Bakery, 1909.

MARY MCDOWELL,
LABOR ADVOCATE

ARY ELIZA McDOWELL (1854-1936) was born in Cincinnati in 1854 and was likely influenced by her father who was active in the anti-slavery movement during the Civil War. The family moved to Chicago soon after the war ended and McDowell was just 16 the year of the great Chicago fire in 1871. Her pastor coordinated relief services for the escaping crowds of people who camped at the edge of the city near the McDowell farm. McDowell's assisting in the distribution of food, clothing, and other relief raised her consciousness about people in need. In 1887, McDowell went off to work as a national organizer for the Young Women's Division of the Women's Christian Temperance Union headed by Francis Willard. Then, in 1890, she returned to Chicago to work at Hull House with Jane Addams and Addams' partner Ellen Gates Starr, where she helped start a kindergarten and women's club.

In 1894, Mary McDowell became Director of the University of Chicago Settlement in Packingtown, one of Chicago's foulest slums. When the University of Chicago started the settlement house in an industrial immigrant to serve as a laboratory for the emerging field of social work and the study of sociology, Jane Addams recommended Mary McDowell for the job. McDowell rented four rooms behind the Union Stockyards and meatpacking plants where she launched the programs. Like her neighbors, McDowell had gaslights, an iron stove, and no running water. Gradually she won the trust of her many neighbors. She served as Director until her retirement in 1929.

Packingtown was an industrial community of 30,000 to 40,000 people located on the northwest side of Chicago. Most residents were recent immigrants from southern Europe.[8] Local residents spoke thirty different languages. Unemployment among adult males ranged from 30% to 50%.[9] The abundant labor supply kept wages low. Children played in streets and alleys, on rubbish heaps and railroad tracks, with toys found in the rubbish dumped on the prairies. Schools were not able to handle all the children. Women worked in factories or at home. In this setting, a settlement made a difference.

An early report defined the purposes of the University Settlement as follows: "The task of the Settlement is to be the wise, understanding, and generous neighbor of a large population of foreign origin who help do the work and share the destinies of Chicago and the United States."[10] The Settlement built a combination gymnasium-auditorium with a stage. In this new facility the Settlement launched a program in music, offered individual lessons, sponsored a 300-voice children's chorus, an adult chorus, and Sunday afternoon concerts. The Settlement brought lectures, art exhibits, literary, and dramatic opportunities to Packingtown. A trained nurse, funded by friends of the Settlement House, visited the sick and taught nutrition and childcare classes to help people from the country know how to care for children in the city.

As she directed these programs, McDowell reflected about the meaning of what she was doing. She was not providing people with a plan, policy, or proposal. She chose to live as a friend and neighbor to bring out the best in all persons and help them see what they held in common. Her purpose was not to hand down a culture to a community of people who came from many cultures. For her, authentic culture was not based on status or economic class. She believed that real culture aimed to bring out the best of human thought and experience and to share this freely. People who could bring out the best in others were, in her words, were "true apostles of equality."[11]

McDowell considered a social settlement to be a clubhouse whose

---

8. *University Record*, University of Chicago, ll:20, August 13, 1897, 167.

9. Howard E. Wilson, *Mary McDowell, Neighbor*, (Chicago: University of Chicago Press, 1928) 29.

10. *Ibid.*, 33.

11. Mary McDowell, "The Social Settlement," Worth M. Tippy, ed. *The Socialized Church* (New York, NY: Eaton & Mains, 1909) 136 and Howard Wilson, *Mary McDowell, Neighbor*, 45.

residents do the duty of citizens. Jane Addams described a social settlement as an effort toward social democracy. Robert Wood called it an attitude of mind. Toynbee Hall, a social settlement in England, was described by Canon Barnett as a center of education, a mission, a polytechnic school, and an expression of philanthropy. Interestingly, the social settlements had no religious requirements for participation, and served community members of many political and religious persuasions. McDowell's motivation, however, was grounded in her Christian faith. She claimed that if she were to use religious terms she would describe the work of a social settlement as "a feeble but honest outward sign of an inner necessity that urges the religious soul to find a way of making real the social ideals of Jesus."[12] But McDowell said that no definition was satisfactory because each was trying to describe an evolving process of life, friendship, and human sympathy. "...It is not the doing of a settlement that interprets it, but the method of living and working *with*, not for, people."[13]

For McDowell, the first and primary concern of religion was to meet human needs, physical and cultural. She treated all people as members of the family of God, and therefore brothers and sisters, regardless of race, class or nationality. McDowell saw her work as that of organizing people for purposes of cultural self-uplifting which would lead to greater equality and social democracy. She believed that people should participate in decision-making about what affected them most directly.

The social settlement launched many specific programs that served the community. It provided food, clothing, shelter, and responses to crisis. It had a kindergarten, adult classes in citizenship and English, vocational guidance and training, a library, and cultural events. The settlement investigated fire hazards following a disastrous fire. It researched housing conditions, family budgets, and health conditions in the neighborhood. It advocated for establishing a juvenile court system, child labor legislation, community centers in local schools, health inspections, and vocational training in public schools. The settlement presented its data before public hearings.[14]

The settlement served needs outside of Packingtown and the Twenty-

---

12. Wilson, *Mary McDowell, Neighbor*, 45. Mary McDowell, "The Social Settlement," *op. cit.* 132.

13. McDowell, "The Social Settlement," *op. cit.* 133.

14. Wilson, *op. cit.*, 46-47.

ninth Ward. To be effective it had to relate to the city of Chicago and so McDowell entered politics in order to obtain city services for her neighborhood. So, for example, since individual homes had no running water, baths, or showers, McDowell took a petition signed by hundreds of residents to the alderman of the ward and persuaded the city of Chicago to build a public bathhouse.[15] It helped that McDowell, Jane Addams, and Harry Ward were members of the City Club of Chicago.[16] They were able to gather support from the business community. McDowell believed that social cooperation was essential to improve human welfare. She joined organizations such as the City Club and the Methodist Federation because the networks could help her work for social betterment.

Other areas of Chicago had regular garbage pick-up, but Packingtown did not have this service. McDowell organized teenagers into Clean City leagues that cleaned alleys and wards and also brought complaints of violations of city ordinances related to city cleaning to appropriate city authorities until they took action.

McDowell also started the first playground in Packingtown. She went to Boston to study this new concept, and then encouraged others who built private playgrounds all around Chicago.

The longer McDowell stayed the more sensitive she became to the enormity of the problems and the quantity of resources needed to address them. She collaborated with the University of Chicago's departments of Sociology and Philosophy to conduct studies. They examined the effect of the stockyards and packing plants on the standard of living in the community. They studied family incomes and sanitary conditions in homes and specifically sanitation and health in relation to tuberculosis and infant mortality. They investigated why half of the children in the school district were performing academically at one or more years below their age group.

McDowell learned that she could not separate problems of individuals and families or community welfare from industrial concerns. The standard of living and sense of human worth and fulfillment were integrally related to conditions of living and employment. By 1900,

---

15. Ibid., 50.

16. Eugene Link, *Labor-Religion Prophet, The Life and Times of Harry F. Ward* (Boulder, CO: Westview Press, 1984) 23. Ward was a member of the City Club of Chicago from 1904-1910.

Packingtown processed 11,635,000 animals a year. By 1904, the packing industry covered 475 acres. McDowell was dealing with an industry giant.

Others before her had tried to obtain better working conditions and lost. In 1879, the Knights of Labor went on strike. Twenty thousand workers lost the strike and their union. In 1886, workers demanded an eight-hour day, but did not get it. In 1894, Eugene Debs led the Pullman Strike, which shut down rail transportation. Butchers engaged in a sympathy strike. A vicious riot ensued, and once again the owners of the packing industry boasted in their ability to end strikes.[17]

When McDowell asked workers what reforms could be initiated, she was met with silence because laborers feared for their jobs. The average wage was only $6 a week, and families absolutely depended on this income. Workrooms were ugly, damp, and cold, and consequently workers were plagued by rheumatism and tuberculosis. Upton Sinclair described the setting in *The Jungle*, a book that inspired a presidential investigation of the industry. Sinclair wrote,

> In a few instances electric fans mitigate the stifling air, but usually the workers toil without relief in a humid atmosphere heavy with odors of rotten wood, decayed meats, stinking offal, and entrails.... In a few cases even drippings from the refrigerator room above trickled through the ceiling upon the heads of the workers and upon the food products being prepared.[18]

The packed meat sent to market contained impurities and contamination associated with the conditions Sinclair described. Workers spent their days in rooms at 38 degrees Fahrenheit with only artificial light, no ventilation, and soggy floors. Some workers stood in boxes of sawdust in an attempt to keep their feet dry. McDowell was concerned about the inhumanity of working conditions and began to speak about this to organizations.

As Mary McDowell interpreted the social problems, she frequently told the story of Maggie Condon. Maggie was a young packing industry worker who tried to save money for her dream of being able to buy

---

17. Wilson, *Mary McDowell, Neighbor*, 75-76.
18. Upton Sinclair, *The Jungle*, (New York, NY: The Viking Press, 1947) cited by Wilson, *Mary McDowell, Neighbor*, 82.

a piano. She was paid by the piece, so to increase earnings she increased her production rate. The foreman's job, however, was to keep wages down. Twice Maggie increased her production to meet high personal goals, and twice the piece-rate was cut, not only for Maggie, but for all the other workers as well. When the third cut was announced, Maggie was ill and exhausted. The young women of the shop demonstrated for better wages, but Maggie was too sick to return to work. The others were blacklisted and not permitted to return to work. Maggie had tuberculosis and, all too soon, she died. She had sacrificed her life for her dream.[19]

Mary McDowell pondered how to proceed with the problem of raising the standard of living in Packingtown. The violence of the railroad Pullman strikes of 1899 roused McDowell to investigate the human cost of labor practices. When McDowell addressed a men's club in Chicago she claimed that women needed labor unions. More women were taking jobs, but they were not admitted to the unions. They were getting lower wages than men for doing the same work. In 1900, McDowell proceeded to help organize the first women's union in the stockyards, the Women's Trade Union League of Chicago, which functioned for women as the American Federation of Labor did for men.

McDowell advocated for the rights of women by writing and speaking for their right to enter trades previously held only by men, for their right to work for equal labor legislation rather than protective legislation for women, and for their right to bargain as primary and essential wage earners who needed to support families. She hoped that young working women would expand their image of themselves to hold a larger view that they were "part of a great social movement of making women think, of making women independent so they can care for themselves."[20] Her biggest concern was to persuade people to "think of the welfare of society."

In 1901, a labor organizer named Michael Donnelly came to Packingtown. McDowell supported his efforts. Together they organized laborers to work for improved conditions through peaceful means and collective bargaining. In 1903, McDowell helped found the National Women's Trade Union League. Wages were slowly raised, working con-

---

19. Wilson, *Mary McDowell, Neighbor,* 86-90.
20. Wilson, *Mary McDowell,* 124.

ditions improved, and children stayed in school a bit longer.

By the time of the 1904 strike, the unions claimed that labor was not a disposable commodity but that it was in fact more important than other factors in production and therefore deserved to be treated as a priority. Jane Addams and Cornelia DeBey, a Chicago physician who documented the sickness, poverty, and starvation in Packingtown, met with industrial magnate J. Ogden Armour, to urge him to consent to labor negotiations. The strikers of 1904 won a position at the negotiating table but lost the strike. They were discouraged.

McDowell understood that the gospel called her to work for the welfare of the whole society. She issued a call to union women to join her: "For you are the burden bearers. On you enlightened organized women rests the duty of awakening the helpless ones in the industrial struggle of today."[21]

McDowell and other key Chicago women also called for a congressional investigation of working conditions. The congressional investigating committee worked from 1907 through 1910 and published a 19-volume report of industrial conditions in the U.S.

In 1909, McDowell served as an executive board member of the Women's Trade Union League, which was campaigning for legislation regulating hours of labor for women, a minimum wage, and appointment of women officials to inspect conditions under which women worked. She lobbied for a ten-hour work day with the Shorter Workday Legislative Association. The Illinois state legislature subsequently limited factory work for women to ten hours a day in 1911. In the 1920s, when Congress established a Women's Bureau as a part of the Federal Department of Labor, Mary Anderson, the new department head, credited Mary McDowell for her work in urging Congress to conduct a four-year investigation of industry that resulted in the creation of the Bureau.

Her efforts to improve the quality of life and social conditions in one locality of Packingtown eventually expanded to affect industry and women in the trades at the national level. Her success encouraged the Methodist Federation to work for change at the national level.

McDowell's work on sanitation extended beyond her neighborhood to impact all of Chicago. Sanitation was a life and death matter in

---

21. Ibid, 124.

Packingtown where frame houses on unpaved streets were surrounded by the stockyards, Chicago's open garbage dump, and Bubbly Creek, a dead arm of the Chicago River into which was flushed the waste from the slaughter houses.[22] The odors were horrific. With no garbage service, residents had little choice but to dump their trash near their own homes, inviting rodents and illness. Yet that was far from all. The entire city of Chicago deposited its garbage in Packingtown in an open dump that exposed Packingtown residents to constant stench and disease.

Year after year, community committees collected information about the problem and filed official complaints with Chicago City Hall. Little was done until 1909. At last, armed with statistics collected by the University of Chicago, McDowell caught the attention of a judge who had never stopped to think about what happened to the garbage that was hauled away from his house. He cooperated with McDowell by issuing an injunction against depositing Chicago's garbage in Packingtown. In the weeks between when garbage collection in Chicago came to a halt and when it resumed, all of Chicago knew that there was a problem with dumping garbage in Packingtown.

During her public appearances speaking to many civic groups about Chicago's trash problem, McDowell began to articulate the ethical issues surrounding the garbage problem. She repeated her understanding that garbage disposal was not just a scientific and political problem but a human issue. She claimed that a garbage disposal plan that burdened one section of the community with health problems, even though it benefited other parts of the community, was "unjust and undemocratic and unwise for all concerned." Though the entire city profited by having a meat supply provided by the stockyards, "the health of the entire city was menaced by the toleration of such conditions as existed in Packingtown."[23] Chicago eventually built a waste reduction plant and then used processed garbage to develop a new waterfront on Lake Michigan, but even that was a temporary measure.

McDowell had made important discoveries. Simply changing the location of a problem did not resolve the problem. It was unfair and thus impossible, she claimed, for others to enjoy prosperity while one

---

22. Howard E. Wilson, *Mary McDowell, Neighbor* (Chicago IL: The University of Chicago Press, 1928) 25, 141.

23. Howard E. Wilson, *Mary McDowell, Neighbor,* 148 and Hermann Loetze, 10.

CHAPTER 2

part of the community suffered unnecessarily.[24] She believed that the city had the responsibility to guarantee the public health and welfare of all people.

As McDowell became an expert in her field, she had new opportunities to lecture and write. In 1908, McDowell gave an address at the Chicago Training School. She claimed that the task of the social settlement is to bring out the best in people. Settlement members work with a common purpose to accomplish some of the functions of a church, a university, and a home. They don't necessarily agree or need to agree. "We love God and we love our fellow men and Christ himself said that this is the fundamental of religion."[25] She believed that if people worked together for the betterment of the whole community they would be "making the work of the church effective."

In 1908, in a presentation to the first National Conference of the Social Workers of Methodism held in St. Louis, Missouri, McDowell described her passion and motivation. She chose not to belong to any political or religious group because of her greater commitment to work against evil and for good in general. She could not anticipate when or where she would need the freedom to speak or act prophetically against injustice and thus felt it would not be beneficial to be affiliated with a single group or organization. The settlement served as "a center of all the agencies that will strengthen and build up the public institutions already at work."[26] The public agencies could work for the goal of social betterment. Rooted in the community and bonded by neighborly acts, the settlement would lead people to City Hall, juvenile court, hospitals, and to agencies that could cooperate to help people in trouble because of poverty, vice, ignorance, and inexperience. Settlements could be influential and forceful in city life because of their direct familiarity with social problems and ability to continuously shape policy to meet needs of the neighborhood. Intimate knowledge of urban neighborhoods helped early leaders in the social gospel movement shape their vision, theology, and political style.

McDowell valued the social settlement for its role in enabling people to "form new moral judgments as to what is right and wrong, where

---

24. 1 Corinthians 12:26. "If one member of the body (community) suffers, the whole body feels pain." CEV.

25. *Deaconess Advocate*, 23:6, June 1908, 5-6.

26. Wilson, *Mary McDowell*, 142.

we have been in such painful doubt."[27] McDowell worked with social settlements, churches, civic organizations and City Hall to re-shape policies for the public good.

In 1910, McDowell wrote an article for MFSS entitled "The Helpless in Industry" that was packed with distressing facts about industrial workers. In this collection of articles by leading Federation members and social service agency executives, McDowell's was unique. Other articles were scholarly, generalized, or sermon-like, covering such subjects as "The Social Message of the Prophets," "The Social Ministry of Jesus," "The Labor Movement," "The Salvation of the Vagrant," "The Needy Child," and "Social Service in the Rural Church."[28] McDowell's documented and investigative approach to social service characterized this and other contributions of the women founders of MFSS to the development of a radical approach that followed in the 1920s.

Mary McDowell was observant of situations that might have been overlooked by someone less attentive to their meaning. One January day in 1913, McDowell looked out her window to see a young Slovakian bride enter the saloon across the street. Late in the evening McDowell found wedding guests dancing with the exhausted bride. A saloon was the only place where dancing was allowed. This prodded her to begin to think that perhaps if the settlement were to provide a dance hall it would be "a means of grace in a city's life." Whereas others simply considered dancing sinful, McDowell saw the matter in more complex terms, understanding the cultural and human aspects of dancing. Here was an opportunity to change thinking and bring out the best in a community.

McDowell kept thinking outside the box when she considered the labor of children in industry. A family's financial hardship was not sufficient reason to expect such sacrifice from children, she maintained, but would be far better resolved by paying more adequate wages to adults. McDowell began to think about protecting children "from the grip of the factory" until they were at least sixteen years old. She wanted to make play a part in public education and dreamed of opening school facilities for recreational purposes as well as for vocational training. Borrowing from the title of one of Jane Addam's books, McDowell saw an "ancient evil" and wanted to help people form a "new conscience."[29]

---

27. Wilson, *McDowell*, 145.

28. Harry F. Ward, ed. *Social Ministry* (New York, NY: Eaton & Mains, 1910).

29. *Deaconess Advocate*, 28:9, September 1913, 4.

For example, when she realized that provisions for the popular celebrations of Thanksgiving and Christmas came at the price of young girls working fifteen hours a day and more for weeks and then collapsing in exhaustion when the days came to be thankful, [30] she realized that the choices and pressures of the religious celebrations had the effect of maintaining poverty. In such myriad ways, McDowell set out to try to understand the root causes of the disease of poverty in the U.S. in order to work to better the human condition. One of the best places to understand how complicated systems work, she realized, is in one's own backyard and in one's own neighborhood.

STUDY QUESTIONS

1. Do you know a place with problems similar to some of those in Packingtown? Describe the problems that you have observed.
2. Describe what it feels like to be a person receiving help. What are some strengths and weaknesses of charity? What might be ways to get around the problems? Do people of means have more responsibility to help others?
3. What did Mary McDowell do to address problems of poverty in Packingtown?
4. Mary McDowell claimed that the first and primary concern of religion is to meet human needs, physical and cultural. Do you agree? Why or why not?
5. "Some attitudes and practices that have been accepted and approved in the past become unacceptable and untenable in the present." Do you agree? Why or why not?

---

30. Ibid., 6.

Isabelle Horton (left) greets a friend, 1909.

Photo of deaconesses from Hilda Steele's Memory Book, 1909.

Isabelle Horton,
Treasuring Human Life

3

I SABELLE HORTON, 1842-1933, was a school teacher in Michigan at the time she read a *Deaconess Advocate* and felt God's call to give her life in service as a deaconess. Though she was already 42 years old, in 1894 she entered Chicago Training School, a school that usually admitted single women between the ages of 18 and 40 but made an exception for Horton. She took the two-year course of study leading to a diploma. She studied general history, church history, missions, nursing, public health, and the Bible, as well as techniques for teaching the Bible. After completing her supervised field work in social service, she was consecrated as a deaconess. Horton took seriously her commitment to Christian living. Like other deaconesses, she made the decision to live on a small stipend rather than a regular salary.

While at the Chicago Training School, Horton demonstrated journalistic ability, assisting Lucy Rider Meyer and Josiah Meyer with writing and publishing the monthly magazine *The Message and Deaconess Advocate.* In 1895 she wrote a monthly column addressed to children that described deaconess life and inspired children to help others with acts of Christian service. In 1896, during Lucy Rider Meyer's prolonged illness, Horton edited the magazine. Then, from 1898-1903 Horton served as Assistant Principal of the Chicago Training School. In 1899, she also became Superintendent of the Deaconess Home, a residence for deaconesses, in Chicago. From 1903-1913 Horton worked for Halsted Street Institutional Church, founding and directing a settlement program there. In 1909, she also was employed half-time as secretary of the Methodist Deaconess Association. Horton continued to write many articles for the *Deaconess Advocate* through 1912, and after that, less frequently.

In 1914, she reported on her work as Superintendent of the Epworth Deaconess Home and Settlement and the Epworth Home for Girls in St. Louis, Missouri. At the Epworth Home she supervised seven church visitors, a Travelers' Aid, a District Nurse, an Evangelist, and four Home Workers.[31] Horton worked as a deaconess for 25 years before she retired in 1919. She died at Agard Rest Home in Lake Bluff, Illinois in 1933.

Isabelle Horton brought a keen analytic mind, an ability to write and organizational skills to her years of service as a deaconess and through involvement in the Methodist Federation for Social Service. Mentored by Lucy Rider Meyer and the Chicago Training School, Horton's thinking about her faith and work changed over time. As a writer, she held positions that were influential for thousands of readers, especially in Methodist circles.

As her thinking changed, she brought others along. For example, in her earlier years as a deaconess, Horton insisted that wealthy people have a responsibility toward those who are poor. She considered that one avenue of recourse for urban problems would be for people of wealth to make reforms because they have more abilities and are in advantageous positions to do so.

As time went by, she claimed that living out the gospel meant gathering community groups as well as individuals to serve the needs of the community. Horton went on to look for the root causes of urban problems. She believed that although secular social service programs such as Hull House were very effective, mission service provided more lasting impact in people because it addressed the heart of their identity, their character, and their faith values for life. But she questioned what would change the values and attitudes of those who were in power?

No longer convinced that making solid, persuasive arguments was sufficient to accomplish social change, and no longer sure that people would want to do the right thing simply because they are good at heart, like McDowell, Horton organized. Part of that organizing included her

---

31. Isabelle Horton, *Deaconess Advocate,* 29:5, May 1914, 11.

work with the Methodist Federation for Social Service where she held office on the general council and worked with a regional group.

Isabelle Horton gradually wakened her own consciousness, and then the awareness of others, to the need for a radical commitment that goes to the roots of the problems of evil. She awoke to one of the most fundamental meanings of the gospel, and how Christians are called to work and speak prophetically in deeds lived out, not just words preached.

Horton held an influential position in the deaconess movement. As associate editor of *Deaconess Advocate* in 1897, Horton introduced a change in the publication. In addition to heart-warming stories of the ways that deaconesses helped people in poverty, Horton added editorial opinions and columns about improving social conditions. In her first signed article, she responded to something President Theodore Roosevelt apparently had recently said, perhaps recommending that the poor go get jobs. She expressed frustration with the way wealthy people would tell poor people simply to go and get work. She asked how this was possible when factories were locked. "If a man does not give back to the world value received, he is a pauper, whether in broadcloth or fustian. There is this difference: the man in broadcloth can afford to wait; the man in fustian [corduroy] starves."[32]

Horton made the case that people have a right to be discontented when faced with overbearing power. She observed that conditions which foster discontent—inequities and injustices—feed an attitude of bitterness.

Horton believed that the effectiveness of deaconesses and others who work for a better society is directly related to their ability to influence industrial systems as well as provide direct services for the poor. She noted that, with the new editorial policy, the *Deaconess Advocate* would report on the deaconess movement, social problems, "the neglected masses, [and] the aggressive efforts of the Christian church."[33]

Horton's biblical theme for her work as a deaconess was "Bear one another's burdens." (Gal. 6:2). She could see how hard it was for the poor people of the inner city to deal with problems and crises, especially when they were hungry, but claimed that for "the strong, the rich, and the successful" there is another way of bearing one another's burdens to

32. *Deaconess Advocate* 12:3, March 1897, 3.
33. *Deaconess Advocate,* 12:6, June 1897, 8.

fulfill their discipleship as Christians. She noted that power is a sacred trust and should be used for the good of humanity.[34] Her 1904 book, *The Burden of the City*, she elaborated on the call to persons who "have" to share in the problems of those who "have less."

Central to Horton's faith was her discipleship to Jesus who modeled a higher law of love and service. "True Christianity, incorporated into politics and business and society, will eternally reform social conditions—nothing else will," she declared.[35] At the same time Horton treasured the good news of Jesus Christ which she knew also spoke to individuals. She urged women to answer God's call to become deaconesses. She wrote with passion about how Christians should live with intention and purpose, choosing, not drifting their way, through life, and putting money and actions to work where their heart responded to God's call. No treasure is more precious than one's life, she claimed. Each woman has one life to give to God. It should be used to bring the "quickest and largest returns in souls saved and work done for God."[36] She urged people to make personal sacrifice to advance God's work. The sacrifice of the deaconess work, essentially unsalaried, but with housing and food provided, she felt opened hearts and doors to people the deaconesses sought to serve.

Mary Agnes Dougherty, in her doctoral dissertation "The Methodist Deaconess, 1885-1918: A Study in Religious Feminism," noted that Horton made a strong appeal to Christians to lead a life of service and sacrifice. Dougherty did not develop a case for Horton's gradual shift in social analysis toward advocating major communal and civic policy changes. Yet Horton came to realize that major changes required more than individual commitments.[37] Her early concern for reform, an approach which works for changes within the social system, gave way to radical visioning, which aims to re-conceptualize and rebuild a social system from different premises.

The encounter of deaconesses with limitations around traditional women's roles and values contributed to her awareness. The *Deaconess Advocate* gave examples of the struggle that deaconesses faced with

---

34. *Deaconess Advocate*, 12:3, March 1897, 3.

35. *Deaconess Advocate*, 12:3, March 1897, 4.

36. *Deaconess Advocate*, 12:8, August, 1897, 8.

37. Mary Agnes Dougherty, "The Methodist Deaconess, 1885-1918: A Study in Religious Feminism," Ph. D. Dissertation, University of California, Davis, 1979, 156.

the changing roles of women. In one mining town a strike extended unabated through long months and the pastor went away to solicit aid for the starving, freezing members of the community. Horton described what happened to the deaconess who filled in for the pastor.

> The deaconess had OCCUPIED THE PULPIT in an emergency, assisted in the Leagues and Sunday school, and filled in the remaining hours of the Sabbath visiting the sick, and clothing such of her little flock as she found in immediate need. For "Is it not lawful to do good on the Sabbath day?"[38]

The fact that the deaconess preached is reported as incidental to the main theme of the story that the deaconess was serving a distressed mining community. There were a few preaching women, but not many. Perhaps, considering the emergency absence of the minister, the deaconess viewed her role more as that of Suzanna, the mother of John Wesley, who carried on worship services in her home during her preacher-husband's absence in the early 1700s in England.

The deaconesses were beginning to enter a traditionally male-occupied vocation. Their ministries and biblical training led them to be next in line to fill Sunday pulpits, a task heretofore reserved only for men. Horton discussed the fact that deaconesses were doing "ministries" and as such were "ministers." She noticed a difference between supplementing the work of the pastors, or helping them, and complementing their work. She argued that deaconesses did not make the work of the pastors better, but more full and finished. Yet her bottom line was this: "*The whole work of the church can never be done while the class set apart for special service is composed of men only.*"[39] The deaconesses were not ordained by the church, but Horton said, "...they are ordered by God, and that makes them an order."[40]

The deaconesses engaged in some elaborate redefining of their changing understanding of ministry which challenged established definitions and roles. As assistant principal of the Chicago Training School, Horton participated in this discussion. Deaconesses began to realize that they could not fit their new understanding into the old framework, and

---

38. *Deaconess Advocate,* 13:1, January 1898, 1.
39. *Deaconess Advocate,* January 1898, 6. Emphasis added.
40. Ibid., 7.

at that point they began to argue for full ordination rights for women.[41] Horton's concerns as a deaconess ran into boundaries with the issue of women's ordination in the church.

Deaconess and social settlement workers faced another huge barrier to change. One might expect that in a democracy, political processes and leaders would help resolve social problems such as those faced by Chicago and Packingtown. Horton watched what happened to Jane Addams and politics in Chicago's Nineteenth Ward. Events shattered her trust in political processes. The significance of this story is that it provided a wake-up call to deaconesses and social settlement workers that they could not count on an educated public electorate to support public policies that would benefit the whole community.

Hull House was located in Chicago's Nineteenth Ward where eighty percent of registered eligible voters were Italians. Italian immigrants moved to the U.S. in large numbers in order to improve their economic circumstances. They wanted to get ahead, but not all means of economic advancement were equally honest or legal. There was an Irish boss named John Powers who provided services which residents needed, but who was corrupt in his dealings. Ward politicians such as Powers normally retained their political power by providing jobs for their constituents. In 1898 nearly one-third of the voters, or about 2,600, were on the public payroll. They worked for the utilities, street car companies, and railroads in jobs obtained through franchises from the government. These workers felt a debt of gratitude to John Powers, the Irish boss who had provided the jobs. Unfortunately, the franchises were poorly negotiated. Public services were in bad shape. Incomes were low. Although some children attended public schools, there was no room for another 3,000 children of school age who lived in the community. Sanitation was terrible. There was no garbage service. The community had no parks. Powers was not doing a good job for his constituents.

In 1895, Hull House Men's Club selected one of its members, Frank Lawler, to run against one of Powers' followers for the position of

---

41. Ordination for women was granted by the Methodist Episcopal Church in 1924. It did not include conference membership, full clergy rights, the right to an appointment, or participation in the itinerant system with other ministers. Generally, married women were not allowed to be ordained because it was assumed that their commitment to their husband would not permit them to give full effort to the church.

alderman. Lawler won the election, but within a short time joined the corrupt officials led by Powers.

The women of Hull House believed that public services would not improve while Powers was in office. In 1896 Hull House helped the Municipal Voters' League campaign for clean government. Skillfully, Powers organized his opposition and won re-election.

Since the election results indicated that a good candidate could sway votes, in 1898, Jane Addams, who was the power behind the initial efforts to reform the politics, tried again to defeat Powers. She had the support of new organizations, including several Italian language newspapers. Powers, however, won re-election by a landslide. This third political defeat in four years led Addams to pull out of local and national politics. Addams, though convinced of the merits of democracy as the highest form of government, was not prepared for informed voters to willingly and knowingly elect corrupt officials. Given these circumstances, the task of reform seemed impossible.

Yet for all that, the failure of reform politics in Chicago clearly radicalized articulate women leaders such as McDowell, Addams, and Horton. Given the difficulties of political reform, Horton chose to speak out for reform of the economic system. She believed that if enough people could see the ethical mandate to change the economic system so that workers would receive "a fair, just and equable share in the product of the combined industry," this reform would have a positive impact that could help resolve many other social problems.[42]

Despite the failure of political reform in Chicago's Nineteenth Ward, the Deaconess movement was making significant changes using other methods, specifically working to change attitudes in the culture. Because of the deaconesses now working in cities across the country, Methodist churches were developing a new understanding of the gospel call to mission and service right in their own backyards.

Isabelle Horton was one of the key persons telling the story that helped church members gain a new perspective. Horton began writing about social conditions and the power of the gospel to bring people together to work for justice.

---

42. *Deaconess Advocate*, 17:7, July 1901, 6.

STUDY QUESTIONS

1. "The mainstream of society was caught up in materialism, not in cultivating spiritual values or developing human character." Does this description fit today's society? Explain.
2. What are some of the conditions which foster discontent and feed an attitude of bitterness?
3. Horton's biblical theme for her work was "Bear one another's burdens." Galatians 6:2. What do you think she meant by this?
4. How would you "go to the roots of the problems of evil?"
    a) Examine bureaucracies to see why they aren't doing their job.
    b) Study nations that go to war.
    c) Throw out the politicians and start a new political party.
    d) Explore the deep-seated psychological reasons why our culture is breaking down.
    e) Analyze human pride, power and greed.
    f) Follow the money.
    g) Other. Explain.
5. Imagine and describe what a society might be like if it were modeled on "a higher law of love and service."
6. Why might you decide to make sacrifices as part of your life and work?
    a) To open hearts and doors to the people you seek to serve.
    b) To reform social conditions.
    c) To avoid drifting your way through life.
    d) To give your life to God.
    e) Other.

Articulating the Social Gospel

To UNDERSTAND THE social gospel involves knowing the way it engages social problems. Among the women in the Methodist Federation at its inception, social gospel thinking was laid out most clearly by Isabelle Horton. As the primary writer and editor publishing in a magazine with a circulation that crested at 32,000, Isabelle Horton had enormous influence on the dissemination of the social gospel among Methodists at the turn of the century. Technically, the *Deaconess Advocate* was still under the editorial control of Lucy Rider Meyer but in practice, Horton selected or wrote much of the content. She also published her own book, *The Burden of the City*.

In dealing with the overlapping problems of immigration, industrialization, and urbanization that plagued the late 1800s, Mary McDowell worked for social change through labor organizing, politics, and social settlement work. Bertha Fowler's springboard of the social settlement specialized in direct aid and community organizing for mutual self-help in order to effect change.

Belle Horton had another gift. Horton used the power of the written word to persuade Methodists to work for community change and justice. Her purpose was to help people understand what it meant to be Christian in a complex society struggling with poverty and massive injustices. Her writings and those she selected for inclusion in the *Deaconess Advocate* form a pattern in the presentation of the social gospel. To the extent that she could motivate local groups such as congregations and women's societies to support deaconesses, she was helping to raise up a grassroots movement for social change. For example, deaconesses began to influence the way many people in the U.S. understood human rights, democracy, freedom, and responsibility. Her goal of winning support for deaconesses work carried with it these broader implications. We turn now to explore what Horton was writing and publishing in order to understand the relationship of these concepts to the development of the radical social gospel.

Even short news items contained the seeds that Horton was planting. By 1901, the *Deaconess Advocate* published a monthly section on "Present Day Questions." Nuggets of information gleaned from a wide range of sources helped deaconesses around the nation keep up with new developments. Occasionally short items questioned assumptions underpinning the social order.

In July, 1901, one news brief cited an article on "The Distribution of Wealth." The *Methodist Review* was quoted as declaring that Christianity faced a new problem, that of discovering "the law of distribution of surplus wealth." While the deaconesses were working with the urban poor, many of them immigrants, some wealthy Methodist congregations were financially supported by barons of industry. Fabulous sanctuaries dotted American cities. The wealth of industry, earned at the price of widespread poverty, built sanctuaries with beautiful stained glass windows and huge pipe organs. Horton planted a doubt, a question mark, around the distribution of economic resources.

The *Deaconess Advocate* carried an article by Lyman Abbott on "The Rights of Man," quoted from the *Outlook*, a publication interpreting Methodist mission work. Abbott argued that certain basic human rights are needed to form a just society. "Every man has a right to the product of his own industry," Abbott declared. Each person invests a portion of their life in their work. If a social structure prevents people from earning a daily living, it is an unjust organization. He commented that if such a structure fails to adequately pay for work, taking "so much from one class that it leaves practically nothing for the [other] class, or leaves them but a mere pittance" is an unjust organization. A worker has "a right to a fair, just and equable share" in the earnings of a company. Abbott was finding that society was not just.[43] The suffering in the cities was fomenting a rising new ethical awareness. Horton wanted Christians to understand that their faith should not be complacent but

---

43. *Deaconess Advocate* 17:11, November 1901, 6.

actively concerned about wages.

Timely topics in the *Deaconess Advocate* provided a steady diet of social comment on how Christians go about transforming society. One of these items was a brief note about an assassination committed by an anarchist, who presumably hoped to accomplish a political point by murdering an opponent. Horton editorialized, "It is by more and better practicing rather than more preaching that society will be saved."[44] She argued that the role of the church in social transformation must go beyond preaching to a real living out of the gospel. The whole mix of views articulated in the *Deaconess Advocate* began to present a picture of a new path in social service that came to be known as the radical social gospel.

Horton was exploring and discussing root causes of social problems. Like Mary McDowell, she advocated the use of social sciences in addressing urban problems and urged people to take the more radical view of looking beyond present issues for causes. Horton wrote,

> When we see poverty, intemperance, wretchedness, we should learn to look beyond it for the cause, and as we shall find the forces which drag down are manifold, even so must be the forces that lift up. ....Everything which improves the physical, intellectual or social nature is also a step somewhere on the ladder that leads up to God.[45]

In this way, Horton questioned the underlying assumptions on which social practices were based.

In 1902, she reported the fact that one-fifth of all workers in Chicago's factories, sweat shops, and stores were children. She questioned the wisdom of the state in allowing such a sacrifice of children, such a squandering of the opportunity and possibilities of so many future citizens, in the cause of supporting their needy families. The short term gain of earning a few more cents every day to support a family would not pay off in the long run when one considered the harm being done to children's health and education.

By 1904, the Deaconess movement, social settlements, and social

---

44. Ibid., 6.
45. *Deaconess Advocate*, 17:11, Nov. 1901, 6.

workers had come into their own. About a thousand deaconesses were serving in the U.S. A network existed which was working to spread the social gospel. These people knew that social systems, not just individuals, needed the good news of Jesus to overcome sin and injustice. The *Deaconess Advocate* documented and celebrated the incredible expansion of the deaconess programs: sixteen years after the General Conference authorized consecration of deaconesses, there were an astounding ninety deaconess homes, eight rest homes, twenty three hospitals, and twelve orphanages.[46]

By 1904, Horton interpreted the crisis in the cities to the nation with her first book. Horton examined materialism in the U.S. and the way the people who purchased goods participated in the cycle of manufacturing and marketing that was undermining the nation's respect for its own workers and citizens. Horton's new book, *The Burden of the City*, was published by the Woman's Home Missionary Society to serve as the interdenominational home mission study course. It was recommended reading for Christians from many churches all over the U.S. This tremendous opportunity helped Horton influence the thinking of thousands of churchwomen in cities, towns, and rural areas.

One hundred years ago the U.S. was still largely a rural nation. Most Methodist churches, located in every county in the nation, were small rural congregations. The church had very little awareness of the problems of the cities and the nature of mission work.[47] Horton hoped to educate people about the problems and also about her developing understanding of Christian theology and mission in the city. Concerned about the materialism of the nation, she wrote:

> There is one power, and only one, that can redeem these masses, and, saving them, save our cities and our nation from the materialism into which they are drifting... This is the Gospel of the Lord Jesus Christ.[48]

For Horton the question was not simply whether the church would

---

46. *Deaconess Advocate*, 24:11, November 1909, 9.

47. This situation has now reversed with more people living in cities having little awareness of rural problems.

48. Isabelle Horton, *The Burden of the City* (New York: Fleming H. Revell Company, 1904) 39-40.

save the masses but whether the church could save itself—by giving itself for the world. Horton believed that the key to the life of the church was its power to impart life to people around it who were numbed by suffering or oblivious to it. *"When it ceases to give life it ceases to live."*[49]

Horton observed a religious debate underway in social settlement work. The question was whether or not to use social settlements to encourage people to become Christians. Horton cautioned against viewing social service programs as bait for evangelizing. She felt that it would backfire if people were required to meet religious criteria in order to qualify for the services and outreach of deaconesses. She felt that the programs were valuable and would help build a more righteous society. "An honest working man does not want alms but justice," she declared.[50] The core issue was justice. Injustice prevailed in daily deceptions, which is why Horton believed that social settlement workers needed to know, for example, just how much chalk and water was added to milk. Pressure from deaconesses could help stop the vendors from cheating people.

Jane Addams refused to use Hull House as an opportunity to press Christianity on people served by the settlement house. Clients came from many backgrounds and religious faiths. Addams regularly lectured at the Chicago Training School, to the disgust of several trustees of the school, who considered Addams to be secular and unchristian because of her position. Some church leaders did not agree with Jane Addams' philosophy of running a social settlement without religious classes, but Horton could see that this choice enabled Addams to serve Protestants, Catholics, and Jews of the neighborhood without discrimination. Addams felt that her work was religious because she was accomplishing good.[51] Horton wished that Addams were willing to use more explicitly Christian appeals to address social problems.

Horton declared that the gospel "is the greatest uplifting force known."[52] She distinguished between a settlement which aims to better "the whole environment of the poor" and missions which begin from the premise that reformation of the individual's heart and life is the starting point for reformation of society. She felt that the gospel of

---

49. *Ibid.*, 42.
50. Isabelle Horton, *The Burden of the City*, 35.
51. *Ibid.*, 61-62.
52. *Ibid.*, 65.

reform needed to be heard by industrial magnates who kept so many millions of Americans in poverty.

Horton thought that the church had created a false dichotomy between sacred and secular. She wanted to help people understand that life cannot and should not be divided into such neat categories. Whenever the world addressed issues of doing right in the manner of Jesus' loving and concern approach, sacred and secular were inseparable.[53] The sacred, or holy, is after all encountered in the wholeness of God's world.

Horton saw that when people engaged reciprocally, relationships were stronger, and the stronger the relationships, the more Christian charity flourished. Today some might say, "What goes around comes around." When the actions of some people bless others, those who have been blessed are more likely to help others.

Concluding her book, Horton showed how the cooperative work of the deaconesses, factory owners, educators, lawmakers, and social service agencies could work together for mutual benefit and social betterment. She believed that a spirit of cooperation and goodwill would command the changes needed to relieve the poverty and misery of the masses of people in the cities. She wrote that Christ-like love is "the lever to lift them into a better life."[54]

Christ-like love reached into dozens of dusty corners of life which she brought to the attention of the readers of the *Deaconess Advocate*. Over a three year period, the *Deaconess Advocate* educated deaconesses and readers in local congregations about dozens of social issues. The list is comprehensive.

---

53. *Ibid.*, 39.
54. Isabelle Horton, *The Burden of the City*, 190.

Deaceness Advocate Social Issues 1906-1908

Prostitution
White slaves
Shop meetings
Starvation
Poverty
Miner's wages
Employment for
   insane
Sweat shop diseases
Prejudice
Italian immigrants
Railroad accidents
Italian farmers
Juvenile homes
Poor young
Working girls
Victims of saloons
Flower gardens in
   cities
Animal disease
Women immigrants
Ghetto charities
School buildings
Abolishing opium
Penny theaters
Negro education
Rickets and poverty
Class spirit
Proposed Fed. Dept.
   of Health

Employment for
   insane
Sweat shop diseases
Floating hospital
Consumptives
Industrial slaves
Scholarships
Reduce child labor
Forest rangers
Suicides
Supreme Court on
   unchurched
   children
Social settlements
Health in the home
Camp Goodwill
Vacation schools
Sunday closing of
   saloons
Crowding in the
   cities
Higher rent
Yellow journals
   (tabloids)
Preschools
Insurance
Child labor law
Political rights for
   children
Tax base for schools

Tuberculosis camp
Sunday laws
Flats
Sweatshops
Cooperative hotels
Labeling of food
Accidents to workers
First aid
Tramps
Fresh air cottages
   (TB)
Women's labor
Instruction of adult
   blind
National school
   gardens
Americanizing the
   alien
Life history of a boil
Anti-Saloon League
Reform of criminals
Billboards
Infant nutrition
National unemploy-
   ment
Boy drifters
Alcohol and disease
Prevent disease
Helicon Hall
   cooperative
   community

The number and variety of topics show the deaconesses' breadth of interest in social conditions and social betterment. They speak volumes of the sacred and secular being joined in Christians' concern for wholeness and the fulfillment of persons and society.

Horton continued to write for the *Deaconess Advocate* while serving Halsted Street Methodist Episcopal Church. Though she had a keen mind for social issues, she did not lose touch with the personal call of the gospel. With touching sentiment, she described how one family with meager resources reached out to help another.

> You go into a little home of two bare rooms and find that they have taken in a stranger, a poor woman turned out on the street for rent. There is but one bed, and the husband gives the stranger his place and sleeps on the floor. How many times have we sent the wanderer on rather than disturb our immaculate guest room?[55]

Horton was intimately concerned about the needs of the 90,000 people of her parish which included 16,000 children under the age of 15 living within four blocks of Halsted Street Church, with no park and no playground.[56] She carried stories with her wherever she traveled. In Denver, addressing the 1905 International Epworth League Convention of Methodist young people (high school to age 30), she spoke on "The Crisis in the Cities." Horton described crowded dingy houses of the city, large numbers of saloons, small toddlers on the front steps of homes right next to the sidewalk, the many foreign languages, sparse rooms and tables without food—in essence, a dismal atmosphere in which people spent their lives. Horton appealed to young people to see that the real sin behind the grim picture was the lack of relationship and caring which allowed this reality to exist.[57] She noted that churches gave a lot of money to send Christian missions to foreign nations, but hadn't yet noticed the opportunity for mission right here in the U.S. when foreigners were immigrating to the U.S. Her experiences were changing her theology and causing friction between her and the wider church.

Horton's criticism of the narrowness of the church's interpretation

---

55. Isabelle Horton, *Deaconess Advocate*, 22:4, April 1906, 8.
56. *Ibid.*, 22:8, August 1906, 12.
57. *Ibid.*, 22:9, September 1906, 9.

of its theology of mission found support in the Methodist Federation. In 1908, Horton addressed the Methodist Federation for Social Service at the Conference of the Social Workers of Methodism. Her paper, along with papers by Mary McDowell, Bertha Fowler and others, was printed in a volume called *The Socialized Church*. Horton's article on "The Deaconess in Social Settlement Work" discussed deaconess experiences with local churches that frustrated her. Several times deaconesses launched nursing services or kindergartens in poor sections of Chicago and were unable to raise support for their work from local churches. Local churches, it seemed, could raise money to hire deaconesses for parish visitation and evangelistic work, but not social work. She felt that these choices short-changed the gospel and the opportunity knocking at the door. Horton lamented the investment of churches in trying to save themselves rather than reaching out to save other people.[58] She wrote, "The deaconess would seek out the lost sheep; the Church would have her rebuild the walls of Zion."[59]

Horton was convinced that the deaconesses offered a significant model for mission, though the results were not necessarily definite or immediate. Horton appealed to the Federation to motivate the church to see the mission at hand in the work of deaconesses in social settlement work. She pleaded for the church not to lose this opportunity. She asked the church to support its trained women:

> I believe now, if this Federation can make it apparent that the Church really desires women especially trained and fitted for social work and will furnish them equipment for such work, they will not only be able to secure them in the near future, but that the demand will give a new impetus to the deaconess order itself....[60]

Regardless of the number of women, or the church's support of trained workers, the question remained about the goal of salvation. Is the nature of salvation material, experienced in human fulfillment that provides food and care in this world? Or is salvation a spiritual event?

---

58. Isabelle Horton, "The Deaconess in Social Settlement Work," from *The Socialized Church*, Worth M. Tippy, ed., (New York: Eaton & Mains, 1909) 154.

59. *Ibid.*, 153.

60. Isabelle Horton, "The Deaconess in Social Settlement Work," *op. cit.*, 169.

Horton did not separate the two.

Horton was concerned about salvation, but argued that people can't save souls because that is the work of the Holy Spirit. She believed that the task of a Christian is to save the environment in which people live so that it is conducive to the development of human character and spirit which are open to receiving what God gives.[61]

> Methodism has come to center all its efforts upon the moment of conversion, placing but little stress upon the years of preparation that make this movement significant, and the careful nurture that is necessary to conserve results.[62]

The work of the deaconess prepared people to receive the good news. The church's role, she believed, would be to "extend its influence so as to touch the social, industrial, and intellectual life of the people."[63]

Horton's radical understanding of the social gospel was grounded in an idealism nurtured by a reading of the life and ministry of Jesus that did not separate what is spiritual or holy from the realities of daily life, an understanding that people could experience the fullness of life and live their way into the reign of God. Horton was describing the experience of opening one's life to the possibilities that God offers. If a society fails to provide conditions that enable human beings to be creative, it is impoverished. Without the basics of food, housing, education, and medical care, the body, mind, and spirit aren't nourished. Horton called the church to create cultural, working, and intellectual conditions conducive to spiritually abundant living. This is the social gospel.

STUDY QUESTIONS

1. Lyman Abbott wrote, "Every man (sic.) has a right to the product of his own industry." What do you think he meant?
2. What are the causes of "poverty, intemperance, and wretchedness?"
3. What are the forces that "lift up?"

---

61. *Ibid.*, 166-167.
62. *Ibid.*, 167.
63. *Ibid.*, 169.

4. Horton was concerned that the nation's drift into materialism was damaging to people and cities. Why? Does materialism contribute to social problems?
5. Horton wrote about the church, "When it ceases to give life it ceases to live." Have you experienced this? Why do you agree or disagree?
6. Why did Horton believe that the gospel "is the greatest uplifting force known?"
7. Choose two topics from the list of titles covered in the Deaconess Advocate. Explain how they might relate to injustice and/or poverty.

Isabelle Horton,
One of the speakers at Milwaukee.
Immediately after the Convention Miss Horton goes
to St. Louis to take charge of the Deaconess
Work in that city.

Isabelle Horton, 1910.

Deaconess programs in Harris Hall, Chicago Training School, 1909.

Bertha Fowler:

Advocate for Social Evangelism

5

BERTHA FOWLER (1866-1952) was born in Lena, in western Illinois, and graduated from Lena High School in 1884. For three years she taught school, first in the country and then in Lena. She graduated from the Chicago Training School in 1888, and went on to attend Garrett Biblical Institute from 1890-93. For three years, she took the same classes taken by men preparing to be pastors, but because she was a woman she was given a certificate, not a degree, and could not be ordained.[64] Given her interests, her graduation from Chicago Training School in 1888, and her studies at Garrett, it is likely that she knew Mary McDowell, Isabelle Horton, and Harry F. Ward, or knew of them, before they gathered at the 1908 Conference on the Social Workers of Methodism and began working together on the MFSS general council.

In 1898, Fowler was working in Chicago when she received a phone call invitation from Mrs. Henry Wade Rogers, wife of the president of Northwestern University, to meet her a week later. She made notes about her meetings with Mrs. Rogers that resulted in a turn in her life.

> February 10, 1898 lunched at Marshall Fields. Made proposition to take superintendency (*sic*) of Marcy Home. Uncertain. Two weeks to think it over.

---

64. *Woman's Home Missions, The Deaconess at Work,* (The publication for Deaconess Work associated with the Woman's Home Missionary Society) XXI:11, Nov. 1914, 17. Bertha Fowler, Box 5, Chicago Training School Archival Collection, United Library of Garrett-Evangelical Theological Seminary and Seabury-Western Seminary.

February 17, 1898 Frances Willard died. Two days later her body lay in state in the Woman's Temple, Chicago. Joined the throng and stood in line for my noon hour and just as I reached the door the hour was up and I returned to work, pledging as I went that I would do anything, go anywhere as I might be led and so notified Mrs. Rogers.

February 24, notified the firm of my decision giving them time to find my successor. NOTICE-Worked for the Jewish firm for $5 a week raised to $6. After paying twenty cents a day for carfare, board and room and laundry I had 80 cents a month for incidentals.

MARCH 9, 1898 about ten o'clock on Wednesday morning I met Mrs. Rogers at Marcy Home and entered upon work for the Woman's Home Missionary Society. $15 a month. No equipment, no training, no experience, scattered work among Bohemians and Jews. SPOKE in churches... [65]

Fowler became a noted teacher, business woman, and evangelist.[66] She worked at the Marcy Home in Chicago from 1898-1904, and then became Superintendent of the Philadelphia Deaconess Home and Settlement from 1904-14. She served a total of forty years as a deaconess.[67]

Fowler was highly educated and had administrative skills and accomplishments. Her pay was not comparable to men of equal education and skill. Yet, as did many Christian women, she felt that the gift of her life and work given to God in Christian service was more valued than being a business woman in a man's world.

In 1907, she worked as field secretary of deaconess work and as assistant to the General Secretary of deaconess work. In 1912-13 Fowler volunteered as a member of the executive committee for the Wom-

---

65. Bertha Fowler, Box 5, Chicago Training School Archive Collection, United Library of Garrett-Evangelical Theological Seminary and Seabury-Western Seminary, Evanston, Illinois.

66. *Woman's Home Missions, The Deaconess at Work,* 17.

67. *14th Annual Report of the Woman's Division of Christian Service of the Board of Missions of The Methodist Church, 1953-1954,* p. 213, and Ruth Esther Meeker, *Six Decades of Service, A History of the Woman's Home Missionary Society of the Methodist Episcopal Church* (Cincinnati, Ohio: Steinhauser, Inc., 1969) 64.

en's Home Missionary Society Bureau on Immigrant Work and was a member of the Philadelphia Committee on Immigrant Work.[68]

From 1914-27, Fowler served at Folts Mission Institute, a training school for missionaries and deaconesses in Herkimer, New York. The 1914 *Women's Home Missions* journal reported, "Miss Bertha Fowler, of Philadelphia, Pa., a woman of rare ability, experience and adaptation to this work, is the president."[69] Fowler's work at Folts continued from soon after it opened until it closed in 1927. Capable women faculty taught a curriculum of "Bible, psychology, pedagogy, history of missions, comparative religions, sociology, domestic science and arts, music, and kindergarten."[70]

Fowler returned to be Superintendent of the Philadelphia Deaconess Home and Settlement from 1928-36. The Philadelphia Settlement provided a large and complex program serving immigrant and working people with a variety of programs that show that deaconesses made a careful assessment of what was needed by the people in their neighborhood. The Philadelphia Settlement sponsored many programs including a:

> thrift shop, dispensary and medical services, a modified milk station, coal yard, savings bank, library, reading room, kindergarten, gymnasium, …Sunday school, daily vacation Bible school, missionary groups, men's clubs, and mothers' meetings.[71]

As Superintendent of the Glen Home, an inner city mission in Cincinnati, Fowler opened a dispensary that provided first line medical clinic services and low cost medicines. She supervised four resident workers and fifteen volunteers.

In 1936, Fowler retired to a home in Milwaukee, Wisconsin, where she lived until 1946. She moved to Ocean Grove, New Jersey, where she died in 1952.

Fowler's gifts for leadership were recognized by other deaconesses when she became field secretary of deaconess work in 1907, preceding Horton. Fowler did not write books or edit a magazine. It was her work

---

68. *Woman's Home Missionary Society Annual Report, 1912-1913*, 20-21.
69. *Woman's Home Missions* XXXI:11, Nov. 1914, 17.
70. *Ibid.*, 17.
71. Meeker, *Six Decades of Service*, 347.

that caught the attention of the Federation. She presented a paper on "The Deaconess as the Pastor's Social Assistant" for the 1908 Conference of the Social Workers of Methodism, which extolled "the intrinsic worth of womanhood in the world's salvation."[72]

Fowler shared with Horton the belief that the church was called to create conditions that nurtured spiritually abundant living. For Fowler, salvation was not only saving for a future life, but enabling men, women, and children to live better now.[73] By living an exemplary Christian life, she wanted her witness to help people pursue high ideals of living, even when life was hard.[74] Because life was tough for so many people in the city, she felt the church must hurry with this urgent task. Living better was more than material well-being such as having food on the table and paying rent. Fowler assessed quality of life in terms of opportunity for meaningful work and hard work done, and cooperation and caring among family members. Fowler believed in extending charity with a watchful eye so that the church would not become "merely a charity organization" whose members seek "loaves and fishes...."[75]

In contrast to McDowell and Horton, Fowler was quicker to judge the behavior of recipients of charity on the basis of whether or not they were being saved although she did provide programs and charitable services to all. However, she held up a yardstick of salvation for every deaconess with a surprising twist that success in their work was to be measured by giving life to others.

> She [the deaconess] has a saved personality. As a pastor's assistant this is power. ...She must win the people to herself and interpret the Christ life if others less fortunate are to join her in the saved life.... Her success will not be measured by the baskets of food or bundles of clothing she distributes, but by the amount of life she gives out.[76]

Fowler wanted to broaden the church's understanding of its task

---

72. Ibid., 192.

73. *Ibid.*, 177.

74. Bertha Fowler, "The Deaconess as the Pastor's Social Assistant," Worth M. Tippy, ed., *The Socialized Church,* (NY: Eaton & Mains, 1909) 139.

75. Bertha Fowler, "The Deaconess as the Pastor's Social Assistant," *op. cit.* 187.

76. *Ibid.*, 191-192.

from doing "evangelism" to doing "social evangelism." She was concerned about providing material necessities and critical of churches focused only on saving souls. This was such a change of dimension in Christian responsibility that she argued that a pastor, usually overworked, needed the help of a deaconess to engage in social evangelism. She wrote, "The Church which was once to save souls needs now to elaborate its program to the salvation of men and women. The time was when men were saved to die, but to save men to live is better."[77] She felt that a deaconess had several important responsibilities. She should visit people and understand their problems, link the rich and the poor in mutual helpfulness, and help families by educating people about parenting and sanitation. She could provide guidance and discipline for families willing to improve their situation, understanding both human nature and social service systems.[78]

Fowler's description of what a deaconess needs to know is further evidence that she was genuinely concerned about the lives and welfare of the "common city dweller."

She believed that a deaconess should know social agencies so that she could make referrals for relief, housing, and food. She should know courts, police, and legal protection to be able to help children. She needed to know how to help people access hospitals, orphanages, mental health care, and shelters. A deaconess should know the cost of groceries, utilities, and rents so that she could tell if people were being cheated, and regulations about marriage and divorce. In sum, Fowler viewed the deaconess as an expert in helping people who have become the victims of "society sharks." A deaconess thus knows "the influences that prevail in the molding of life and character."[79]

Instead of focusing on the church's traditional concern for the salvation of souls, Fowler believed that churches should concentrate on serving the needs of individuals and families. Fowler likely agreed with the common belief of the time that people's misfortunes were related to their ignorance, bad luck, circumstances or poor choices. She did not place responsibility for injustice on the "society sharks," the economic system, or society as a whole. Yet she knew that the church had become

---

77. *Ibid.*, 188-189.
78. Bertha Fowler, "The Deaconess as the Pastor's Social Assistant," *op. cit.*, 188.
79. *Ibid.*, 188-189.

complacent and needed to reach out.

In 1908, Bertha Fowler shared with McDowell and Horton a concern that urban congregations were more concerned with serving the baptized than with ministering to the poor who lived in crowded tenements near the church. The church was more interested in winning new members than in addressing the widespread evils in the social order that kept making poor people poorer. Fowler was supportive of the ministry of institutional churches such as Halsted Street Institutional Church where Horton worked, that was equipped with a gymnasium and meeting rooms that were used by all kinds of community groups. Horton had noted that, on the whole, churches were more likely to move to the suburbs than to invest energy and resources in the local community. Fowler organized Christian service to the urban poor.

McDowell and Horton provided more complex social analysis than Fowler. Fowler was more representative of the majority of their deaconess colleagues. Fowler was not confronting systemic injustice or reflecting on the morality of government or social systems. McDowell and Horton were unusual in their ability to understand complex contributions of urbanization, immigration, industrialization, and economic injustice to the social problems they addressed. Fowler was not.

In her essay in the MFSS volume on *The Socialized Church*, Fowler wrote that she did not perceive herself expanding the role of women, which is surprising, given her theological education equal to that of the best-trained clergy. She was comfortable being a pastor's assistant and maintaining traditional authority relationships between men and women. She seems to have accepted the traditional social gender roles and the economic disparity between rich and poor. Without sensitivity and awareness that critiqued the social systems, she did not take the more radical social stance of McDowell and Horton.

We turn now to the story of the beginnings of the Federation and the participation and leadership of Grace Scriber and Winifred Chappell. The story about the role of women in the Federation and their development of social gospel thinking continues, but the Methodist Federation for Social Service began with very little involvement of women.

STUDY QUESTIONS

1. What does it cost to live a simple, modest life style in your area? What portion of the people who live in your area are poor?
2. Bertha Fowler felt a Christian calling to save people and enable them to live better now. Isabelle Horton commented that only the Holy Spirit can save a person and that Christians should help create an environment conducive to experiencing spiritual fulfillment. Compare their views of salvation and how their different views had different results.
3. Fowler viewed the deaconess as an expert in helping people who have become the victims of "society sharks." Who are these society sharks and victims today?
4. Fowler said that a deaconess knows "the influences that prevail in the molding of life and character." What influences mold life and character today? Who needs to know about these influences? Why?

The faculty and student body of Chicago Training School in front of the school, 1897.

Chicago Training School Class of 1913.

First Row: Gladys Randall, Agnes Young, Emily Cummins, Grace Linfield, Ethel Lasby, (Dammien?), Hettie Still, Harriet Severns, Bertha Zook, Ethel Hancock, Serena Johnson, Helen Fritz, not known.

Second Row: Ida Whitlow, Belle Vinall, Lucy Joslyn, Gladys Wilmuth, Lulu Mae Werner, Blanche Perry Brower, Lucy Rider Meyer, Edith Cox, Mary Ellen Davidson, not known, Rose Bradley, Sadie Robinson, Bernice Adams, Dora Dillon.

Others, possibly not pictured: Ethel Harwood, Annie Burkridge, Birdie Beringer.

FOUNDING THE METHODIST FEDERATION

6

F IVE PROMINENT METHODIST clergy began to discuss the pos-
sibility of starting an organization to promote social service. In
the fall of 1907, Harry F. Ward, Frank Mason North, Herbert
Welch, Worth M. Tippy, and Robb Zaring issued the call to meet in
December to form a new organization.

Frank Mason North, a mission executive for the Methodist Episcopal Church, came from New York City. He knew better than anyone
else the whole scope of Methodist mission work in the United States—
what was happening and what wasn't.

Worth Tippy, a pastor from Cleveland, Ohio, was keenly interested
in the development of the field of social service as it was beginning to
unfold. He served a congregation that had a long history of social involvement. There were tunnels and hideaways dug underneath various
Methodist churches in Cleveland. Slaves headed north to freedom had
spent the night at these illegal stops on the underground railway. Perhaps church members had provided hospitality, but that was long ago.
Tippy cared about poverty and industrialization in Cleveland now. So
he traveled to England by ship specifically to study the Wesleyan Methodist Union for Social Service during a study leave from his pastorate
in Cleveland, Ohio.

Herbert Welch, the President of Ohio Wesleyan University, studied
at Oxford University in England before becoming president of Ohio

Wesleyan in 1905.[80] Ohio Wesleyan was located in an area where predestination was at the center of religious debate. Here the Methodists challenged this predominant thinking, taught primarily by Presbyterians.

A second characteristic of Ohio Wesleyan was its location at the crossroads of shipping and rail transportation for the rapidly industrializing nation. The Great Lakes, the rivers, and the Erie Canal carried cargo east, west, and south through the heart of the nation. Ships were being replaced by trains. Farms were giving way to industries that were creating large urban areas where steel and iron workers labored in poverty.

The problems of the nation came under intellectual scrutiny at Ohio Wesleyan University. As the president of this prestigious university that was at the center of advocating the vital role of Christian responsibility, Herbert Welch stepped forward to help lead the Federation.

Robb Zaring also came from Cincinnati, Ohio. He served as editor of the *Western Christian Advocate*, a highly influential position because every Methodist pastor was expected to read this magazine and it circulated to thousands of church members.

Harry Ward, from Chicago, had begun his career as head resident of Northwestern Settlement, only a block away from Mary McDowell at the University of Chicago Settlement. It may well be that Harry Ward advocated with his male colleagues as they formed the new Methodist Federation to include in its membership his women colleagues in social settlement work and the deaconess movement. In an era of organizations separated by gender, it was unusual that the Methodist Federation accepted women members. Even more unusual perhaps is the fact that Mary McDowell was on the invitation list for the founding meeting of MFSS.

Ward, North, Tippy, Welch, and Zaring signed and sent invitations to the December meeting to 50 men and to Mary McDowell. She was not able to attend. The letter described their intent.

> The Committee has in mind the formation of a society to stimulate a wide study of social questions by the church, side by side with practical social service, and to bring the church into touch with neglected social groups. It is an effort to apply the same and

---

80. Donald K. Gorrell, "The Methodist Federation for Social Service and the Social Creed," *Methodist History*, 13:2, 1975, p. 4.

fervent spirit of Methodism to the social needs of our time.[81]

These Methodists wanted to rekindle the early Methodist tradition of serving neglected and poor segments of the population.

On December 3 and 4, 1907, a group of 25 persons attended the first meeting of the Methodist Federation for Social Service in Washington, D.C. One of the men who came to that meeting was E. J. Helm, the Methodist founder of Goodwill Industries in New York City. The five conveners came from Chicago, Cincinnati, and New York. With intentions to influence national policies, they went to the seat of U.S. political power. These Methodists concerned about social service didn't have cars or airplanes at their disposal. They traveled by train to their organizing meeting, as people did frequently. It was their shared concern for justice that drew them together.

After much discussion, they agreed on the purpose of the organization: *"to deepen within the church the sense of social obligation and opportunity to study social problems from the Christian point of view, and to promote social service in the spirit of Jesus Christ."*[82] The intent of the broadly inclusive purpose statement of MFSS was to establish a broad base of support so that social service goals might quickly permeate the work of the church. Differences in theological perspective were minimized so that members could agree to work together.

The Methodist Federation chose Herbert Welch to serve as president of the new organization. The founders arranged a meeting with President Roosevelt to bring his attention to their concerns for the nation.

As members of the Federation sat down together at the May, 1908 General Conference to strategize how they would introduce their legislation for the church, they decided to formulate a Social Creed. Harry F. Ward penned eleven points on the back of a telegram paper. The Social Creed provided talking points for the church about its call to deal with social problems. General Conference adopted the Social Creed, making it an official position statement of the Methodist Episcopal Church.

The Social Creed took up the same social issues that McDowell

81. Donald K. Gorrell, "The Methodist Federation for Social Service and The Social Creed," *Methodist History* 13:2, 1975, 3-32.

82. Minutes of the Methodist Federation for Social Service, George D. McClain, "Pioneering Social Gospel Radicalism: An Overview of the History of the Methodist Federation for Social Action," *Radical Religion*, 5:1, 1980, 10.

and Horton were addressing in their ministries of social service. The creed began with a concern for equal rights and justice for all. It moved immediately to concern about labor relations in industry. It took up questions of health and safety for workers, and opposed sweatshop conditions where workers who received low pay and worked long hours. It called for the workweek to be reduced to six days and for industries to pay living wages. Finally, the creed called for people to treat others as they would want to be treated. It helped the organization stand for a positive vision.

THE 1908 METHODIST SOCIAL CREED

The Methodist Episcopal Church stands:
- FOR equal rights and complete justice for all men in all stations of life.
- FOR the principles of conciliation and arbitration in industrial dissensions.
- FOR the protection of the worker from dangerous machinery, occupational diseases, injuries and mortality.
- FOR the abolition of child labor.
- FOR such regulation of the conditions of labor for women as shall safeguard the physical and moral health of the community.
- FOR the suppression of the "sweating system."
- FOR the gradual and reasonable reduction of the hours of labor to the lowest practical point, with work for all; and for that degree of leisure for all which is the condition of the highest human life.
- FOR a release from employment of one day in seven.
- FOR a living wage in every industry.
- FOR the highest wage that each industry can afford, and for the most equitable division of the products of industry that can ultimately be devised.
- FOR the recognition of the Golden Rule and the mind of Christ as the supreme law of society and the sure remedy for all social ills.

From the outset the Federation launched an educational campaign using publications. The Federation asked members and friends to write essays about social service, the sources of their views, and the implications of the social gospel. The Federation began by defining social service as the effort to "uplift and transform" community life and re-lationships. Social service also included attention to the social needs of individuals to help people establish supportive conditions for the development of their lives. Social service included aid and assistance for people who were poor, sick, and in prison, especially when combined with efforts to "discover and remove the causes of poverty and disease and crime."

> The goal is social salvation, the deliverance of human society from disease, poverty, crime, and misery; the development and perfection of the institutions of man's associated life; and the construction of a social order that is the city of God on earth.[83]

Social service was not a new concept to the McDowell, Horton, and Fowler who attended their first MFSS meeting in 1908. They had developed their own working definition from their experiences. They were becoming disillusioned, however. McDowell and Horton were starting to doubt the ability of society to achieve social salvation and were looking instead toward bringing together various forms of remedy to cope with ever-changing institutions. Nothing was constant. Immi-grants, child labor, working women, garbage disposal, unemployment, and hunger changed faces but were never resolved. The cycle perpetuat-ed itself, changing its rules, at times becoming insidious. At this point, McDowell and Horton did not write about envisioning alternatives to capitalism or the re-ordering of power structures, but the poverty cycle may have been stirring their thinking.

The Federation looked for ways to be more specific about its task. The members set six objectives.

- The objective for child welfare was to secure for every child the best possible education, adequate recreation, good housing, protection from vice and from industrial exploitation, and to care for depen-dent, delinquent and defective (*sic*) children.
- For public health the objective was to enforce individual responsi-bility for the health of the community and to spread the knowledge of the methods of preventing disease.

---

83. *Social Service*, a pamphlet, Methodist Federation for Social Service, 1908.

- For poverty, to relieve and remove destitution by organized constructive charity work and to discover and remove the causes of poverty;
- For public institutions, to secure the highest standard in all institutions for the care of dependents, defectives (*sic*), and delinquents, by visitation and inspection, by cooperation with public officials, and by legislation;
- For delinquency, to provide the best reformatory treatment for the offender, to aid discharged prisoners, and to discover and remove those conditions which contribute to delinquency; and
- For the worker, to secure in every community one day's rest in seven, industrial safety and workmen's compensation, reasonable hours of labor, and a minimum wage.[84]

These objectives for social service focused on persons and relationships, in contrast to a culture that, as in our time, was intent on making money for industry, corporations, and financial markets.

The first objective of the Federation was to give priority to children, those who were at the mercy of the society and culture into which they were born. The Federation's goal was to help children in poverty, an interesting parallel to the recent Bishops' Initiative on Children and Poverty. The persistence of poverty as a primary social problem provides strong motivation for us to examine different approaches to charity and social change.

J. W. Magruder, a member of the Federation, in an early pamphlet entitled *The Methodist Church in Organized Charity,* defined three forms of charity which he labeled emergency relief, adequate relief, and radical relief. Emergency relief is the first temporary aid which comes before the other two. Adequate relief, requiring time, thought, and skill, aimed at "the physical, moral, intellectual, social and spiritual redemption of any individual or family in distress." Radical relief is the term used to get to the root causes of the distress. It addresses the causes of the bad housing, transmission of disease, child labor, addictions, and breakdown of law. It explores in order to find out what is the evil

---

84. Methodist Federation for Social Service, "Our Immediate Program," 1908, John Milton Huber, "A History of the Methodist Federation for Social Action," Boston University, Ph. D. Thesis, 1949, 76.

that is attacking the life, health, and character of the community[85] By Magruder's definition, McDowell and Horton engaged in social analysis and led in developing strategies of radical relief.

Even though members of the Federation had many different opinions and approaches, the roots of two approaches to social problems were present at its inception. One was a vision of social service that provided adequate relief through gradual reform. The other was a radical vision of a new social order grounded on new principles of equality, justice, and cooperation.

In the early 1900's social gospel leaders believed that reform of social systems could be accomplished within a democratic capitalist system. Before members could embrace a radical vision they had to experience disillusionment with the accepted methods of social change. Some of them eventually concluded that capitalism is fundamentally flawed. William McGuire King discussed this foment among the early MFSS members.

> Still, they continued to hope that a society based on the principles of human cooperation and social justice—principles that most of them found sadly lacking in the social and economic circumstances of their own childhood—could be established. They tended to concentrate on industrial issues because they considered the drift and aimlessness of the current industrial civilization to be the greatest threat to this ideal.[86]

The Methodist Federation began lifting up visions of what society could be, in contrast to a society racked with problems and sobered by the failure of charity and philanthropy to undo the tragic concentration of wealth and power in the hands of a few to the detriment of the many. Their challenge now was to persuade church members of their responsibility as Christians to help shape the social order in order to care for the needs of all people.

---

85. "Our Immediate Program," Methodist Federation for Social Service, 1908, cited by John Milton Huber in "A History of the Methodist Federation for Social Action," 76.

86. William McGuire King, "The Emergence of Social Gospel Radicalism: The Methodist Case," *Church History*, December 1981, 440.

STUDY QUESTIONS

1. The purpose of MFSS was "to deepen within the church the sense of social obligation and opportunity to study social problems from the Christian point of view, and to promote social service in the spirit of Jesus Christ."
   a) Does the church today have a sense of social obligation?
   b) What is social service in the spirit of Jesus Christ?
   c) Is there a Christian point of view? Describe or explain.
2. If you were creating a social creed, what would be one important point to include?
3. What are some of the factors that perpetuate the cycle of immigrants, unemployment, poverty and hunger?
4. What contemporary movements or groups are addressing problems related to immigration, unemployment, poverty and hunger? Describe.

Probably the faculty of Chicago Training School, 1909.
Back row, L: Isabelle Horton; R: Lucy Rider Meyer.

GATHERING MOMENTUM
FOR A NEW SOCIAL ORDER

7

THE CALL TO form the Methodist Federation for Social Service was also a call to action for Christians to help establish a new social order. The founders began by expanding their network and persuading others to share their vision.

The 1908 General Conference adopted the Social Creed that was originally penned by Harry Ward but amended and adopted by the Federation. The creed was accompanied by a four-page report which "stressed the primacy of human values and the necessity of Christianizing human relationships."[87]

Frank Mason North, a member of the Federal Council of Churches' Committee on the Church and Modern Industry, reworked The Social Creed, adding one point. The Federal Council of Churches adopted it as an official statement on December 4, 1908. North prepared a report that named a Christ-centered basis for social service by churches, and emphasized the redemptive work and authority of Jesus: "Christ's mission is not merely to reform society but to save it. He is more than the world's Re-adjustor. He is its Redeemer."[88] North described the mission of the church as being different from other organizations that were concerned for human well-being. First, he said, although the church works to bring about God's reign on earth, life's final fulfillment is with God. Second, the gospel of Christ is not a class gospel. It is for all persons.

---

87. Huber, "History," 95.
88. Donald Gorrell, "The MFSS and the Social Creed," 17.

Third, the church's mission is to reveal the meaning of righteousness, justice, and salvation so that people may be redeemed and these ideals become the principles of the new social order implemented in people's lives. Fourth, the church represents Christ who shows God's love bearing fruit in God's reign lived on earth. For this reason the church should be less concerned with details of services of worship and more concerned with its services to people.[89]

The Social Creed and the founding of the Federation grew out of a sixteen-year history of attempts of Methodists to persuade the Methodist Episcopal Church to think and work in terms of creating a new social order. Since 1892, North had been working to address the problem of the increasing concentration of wealth and power in the hands of a few. North had chaired a committee of five persons named by the New York East Conference of the Methodist Episcopal Church. The committee's task was to develop a petition to General Conference calling for a new social order based on "brotherhood" and on principles of profit sharing and cooperation.

In 1896 Herbert Welch and two others joined North's committee and sent a petition calling for a new social order to General Conference. This time the petition named specific social problems and called for the church to respond. As happened in 1892, the General Conferences of 1896, 1900, and 1904 provided disappointing responses to these concerns. As the dream of a new social order seemed to come no closer, and as the committee experienced resistance to social change, leaders felt called to create a new unofficial channel for action—the Methodist Federation for Social Service.

Dr. Herbert Welch, President of Ohio Wesleyan University, was the first president of MFSS. In his view, the social problems of the day were related to the way Christian faith had increased the perceived value of human life. "The seriousness of a man's lack of comforts, conveniences, opportunities, depends upon one's estimate of the worth of [persons]."[90] Christianity so lifted up the value of human beings that those factors which tear down and destroy or those which enhance life fulfillment became important.

In Welch's 1908 speech before the conference of Methodist social

---

89. Donald Gorrell, "The MFSS and the Social Creed," 17-18.
90. Herbert Welch, "The Church and the Social Need," *The Socialized Church*, 15.

workers he reaffirmed that the church has a record of helping "the weak …the enslaved, the struggling, the disheartened." The core issue was not what had been accomplished, according to North, but whether its mission had been fulfilled. That mission was the mission Jesus claimed from Isaiah—preaching good news to the poor and oppressed, healing the broken-hearted, setting at liberty those who are captives.(Is. 61:1-2, Luke 4:18-19.) "We must present not only a pure gospel for the spiritual [person] but a whole gospel for the whole [person], and a gospel which finds its way into our daily practices."[91] Welch used Jesus' life to illustrate how practical concerns integrate with spiritual life and wholeness. Jesus offered a whole gospel to a broken world. On this foundation, the Methodist Federation was born and continues.

William M. Balch, pastor of St. John's Methodist Episcopal Church in Dover, New Hampshire, and secretary of MFSS, believed that it would make all the difference in the world to the new social order whether it was "founded on the words of Jesus or on the shifting and unstable sands of selfishness and unbelief." He believed that society was headed in the latter direction. For a new social order to be better than the present one, it needed solid grounding in universal principles that lifted up the worth of relationships based on love and justice. He saw big changes occurring and hopeful signs in emerging social movements that offered promise for a better future society. He pointed to the "reorganization of industry on the lines of cooperation…instead of free competition." Balch anticipated increased governmental regulation of private business, socialization of more economic enterprises, and organizing of labor. For Balch, socialists in the U.S., the agrarian movement in Russia, social and economic rejuvenation of Asia, and the American experiment in democracy were positive signs of the unleashing of great possibilities for civilization such as the world had never known. On the other hand, they could also mean the "ultimate overthrow of the civilization that now is."[92]

Balch was concerned that the majority of the people in the cities considered church irrelevant. His response was to preach the social gospel, noting specific major problems with attempts to save society by focusing on saving individuals.

---

91. *Ibid.*, 27.
92. William M. Balch, "The Pulpit as a Social Force,' *The Socialized Church*, 208.

Harry Ward served as the second vice president of MFSS from 1907-1908. Then he became editorial secretary of MFSS with responsibility for publications. Ward was a strong advocate of the labor movement because it offered voice, action, and power to a class of people who historically labored without voice in government, legislation, health, education, or cultural concerns. Ward believed that laborers deserved their share of political power and social control.[93]

Ward served as chair of the Committee on Labor Conditions of the City Club of Chicago. He was organizer of the Industrial Committee of the Churches of Chicago and served as chair of the Commission on Church and Labor of that organization. Through these channels he helped secure social and labor legislation in Illinois.[94]

Ward wrote an article on "The Labor Movement" that was published by MFSS in 1910 in a book called *The Socialized Church.* In this article he cited statistics indicating that the average daily wage in the U.S. was $1.38 while the *per capita* goods produced were valued between $12 and $14 per day.[95]

Ward's arguments defending the labor movement were based on his faith emphasis on the value of human life and the Christian emphasis on relationships. With at least ten million poor in the U.S. at that time, Ward claimed that the unrest of labor was the cry of people who refused to continue to suffer from injustice. He claimed that the real purpose of the labor movement had spiritual implications because it demanded that people be raised above being treated like animals. Human beings should not be forced "to work to the point of exhaustion and to live like beasts," he advocated.[96] Ward believed that the labor movement was a strong religious force because of its idealism, but he thought that it would benefit from "God consciousness, the sense of eternal values, and the obligation of universal brotherhood...."[97]

Worth M. Tippy, first vice president of MFSS, was pastor of Epworth Memorial Methodist Episcopal Church in Cleveland. His congregation organized several committees. One of them, the Social Ser-

---

93. Harry F. Ward, "The Labor Movement," *Social Ministry*, Harry F. Ward, ed., (New York: Eaton and Mains, 1910) 107.

94. John Milton Huber, "History," 93.

95   John Milton Huber, "History," 122.

96. Harry F. Ward, "The Labor Movement," *Social Ministry*, 126.

97. *Ibid.*, 131.

vice Committee, provided relief to persons in the parish who were sick, destitute, old, or unemployed.[98] His church also provided temporary assistance for families referred by the Deaconess Home or by Associated Charities. They worked closely with other social agencies in the community such as the juvenile court, City Hall, hospitals, and the Children's Aid Society.[99] Tippy believed that pastors should not be timid about speaking out on social problems. His sense of boldness about engaging new forms of parish ministry and addressing relevant issues from the pulpit placed him alongside Harry Ward. These two MFSS members were willing to take personal risks as part of their style, engaging social problems of their time.

Most of the men in MFSS were reformists who believed in bringing about the "City of God" on earth through the power of love. Ward and Tippy worked hard to bring about substantive changes. Perhaps they sensed that significant change would not come about without conflict.

In several ways, Mary McDowell and Isabelle Horton had already run into conflict. They had seen avenues for democratically elected politicians to implement social change be crushed when a strong leader like Jane Addams could not change the politics of the Nineteenth Ward. They had witnessed the years of struggle behind trade union organizing. They knew how long and hard social settlements had worked to get garbage service in Packingtown.

By 1901 Mary McDowell and Belle Horton had discounted several theories of social change, as had several other key founders of MFSS. To them, religion was not a matter of personal belief, which, by changing attitudes of individuals, would bring about the better society. They knew that their skills in social work eased social problems but did not resolve them. McDowell's efforts to unite civic and religious organizations had made an impact on problems, but were not adequate. High ideals and good deeds were not sufficient. As with Herbert Welch, McDowell and Horton's understanding of Christian faith emphasized actions lived out in society as well as in individual life. Valuing human life and treating people with Christian love and respect was central to the process of social re-ordering. A new social order was not a one-time

---

98. Worth M. Tippy, "The Organization of a Church for Social Ministry," *Social Ministry*, 235.

99. *Ibid.,*, 239-240.

construction process. Re-ordering and renewing society to keep these values at the center would be a continuous process.

McDowell and Horton focused on relationships with persons, not relationships with the environment. They lived in a century that was anthropocentric, with decisions revolving around people who made the decisions, counting dollar costs but not human consequences or environmental impact. Love, justice, and neighborliness were key concepts in such an understanding.

Horton and McDowell believed that people should make a difference in society. Coalitions of science and religion and of civic and religious groups were essential to the process. Horton suspected that government, big business, and churches were at times in alliance against the values she held at the core of her faith. By 1901, these two women were ready to explore concepts of social reconstruction. McDowell was prepared for the risks of radical action because she had taken unpopular stands. She had risked personal confrontation with the industrialist, Lewis Armour, on behalf of her principles.

Radical visioning is critical of the evil embedded in current social systems. It dreams of what could be better and how. Both the Methodist Federation and the deaconess movement were established outside the traditional structures of the Methodist Episcopal Church. They sought to relate to it and influence it precisely because they had new visions for the church. Thus, although women were excluded from ordination and from participating as church leaders in the halls of church government, they had developed channels through the deaconess movement to provide trained services to the church.

In a similar way to the experiences of the women, the efforts of other social gospel leaders to move the Methodist Episcopal Church to take strong stands on urgent social issues had been thwarted at one General Conference after another. Then, in 1907, a handful of clergy issued the call to form the Methodist Federation in order to educate and lobby the denomination to adopt a social gospel stance.

On November 19, 1908, immediately following the Conference on the Social Workers of Methodism held in St. Louis, Mary McDowell, Isabelle Horton, and Bertha Fowler were elected to the general council of MFSS. A smaller group of seven persons formed the initial executive committee.

The new organization had big dreams and a powerful vision, but not enough money to hire a staff person. Instead the Federation created four committees. The four committees were these:

Social Centers, to consider and promote the establishment and maintenance of social settlements and like agencies under Methodist auspices;

Social Studies, to consider the possible introduction of social topics and text books into the courses of theological schools, colleges, deaconess homes, conferences, etc;

Church and Labor, to consider the present situation between the church and the workingman, and to suggest means for bringing the church into more cordial and effective relations with the labor movement; and

General Conference Reference, to prepare a report for the next meeting of that body in 1912 in response to the four questions assigned to the Federation for investigation in 1908.[100]

Mary McDowell chaired the committee on Social Centers, and thus came to serve on the Executive Committee of MFSS. The Federation wanted to educate and assist congregations baffled by the enormity of the problems of the cities to know how to begin to cope with the pressing issues. The Methodist Federation began its work to redress major social problems.

These committees helped the general council and the executive committee with the work of the organization. In 1911, the Methodist Federation for Social Service started the *Social Service Bulletin*, a quarterly publication, with Harry F. Ward in charge. The *Social Service Bulletin* of the Methodist Federation was launched in 1911 after the *Deaconess Advocate* had already built a broad circulation and was well established as a source of news and information for the Methodist Episcopal Church. The *Deaconess Advocate* was widely read by Methodist deaconesses, Methodist women in local churches, and members of the Woman's Home Missionary Society. It also catered to children with a

---

100. John Milton Huber, *"History of the Methodist Federation for Social Service,* 85.

monthly children's page. The *Social Service Bulletin*, on the other hand, was written for adults, mainly men and women of the Methodist Episcopal Church, focused on developing ways for the denomination to engage in social issues.

The first two issues were devoted to organizational details, but by July 1911, the fledgling publication began to take up the causes that have been themes of the life of the Federation ever since. The first theme was "World Peace." A lengthy article by Ward expressed the concerns of the new organization and launched a campaign to support the concept of a system for international court arbitration of disputes between nations. The idea had been proposed by President Taft and supported by Sir Edward Grey of Great Britain and became a reality with the formation of the World Court. The signers of the MFSS World Peace Statement included all three women founders, further evidence of their active membership and participation.

Signers of the MFSS World Peace Statement, 1911

Herbert Welch	Bertha Fowler	Worth M. Tippy
Homer Folks	Harry F. Ward	J. W. Magruder
E. J. Helms	Mary McDowell	John Williams
Charles M. Stuart	William Balch	George A. Vincent
Edward T. Devine	Isabelle Horton	J. W. Kline
George A. Coe	Frank Mason North	

This document provides evidence that the women had become integrated into the leadership of the Methodist Federation which was now organized to move forward. When injustice was pervasive and when neither political nor economic reform brought quality of life, then it was time for the Methodist Federation to examine the principles needed to create a new social order.

STUDY QUESTIONS

1. Which of the following images for a new social order most accurately describes your vision? Why?
   a) A world in which nations do not go to war.
   b) A society based on equality of all persons.
   c) A family in which members love one another.

d) A society in which people help each other so that no one lacks food, shelter, or basic necessities.

  e) A culture in which people can do whatever they desire.

  f) A society with an economy based on sharing.

  g) A society in which no one makes mistakes or hurts anyone.

  h) Other.

2. Read Luke 4:18-19. Did Jesus fulfill this mission? Explain. Does the church do these things? Explain.

3. What do you think is one of the important social problems today that needs the help of churches? What kind of help is needed? How would you motivate people to take action?

Deaconesses in front of the Mary Delamar Kinnear Monnett building, 1909.

TO-DAY AND TO-MORROW

TO-DAY

To-day, these children come from ill-kept, insanitary homes, the homes of the ignorant poor.   But also

To-day, they are being trained in right methods of house-keeping by skillful, Christian workers.   They are learning to do by doing.

TO-MORROW

To-morrow, we have faith and hope to believe, these same children, older grown, will put into practice the methods they have learned to-day.

To-morrow, we hope to have no *ignorant* poor.

Turning Point

M ARY McDOWELL, Isabelle Horton, and Bertha Fowler stayed
with the Methodist Federation during the first few years, giving leadership on the general council.[101] The women brought
to the Federation connections with two large networks of concerned
allies—the social settlement movement and the deaconess movement.
Two good friends, Grace Scribner and Winifred Chappell, both Methodist deaconesses, now joined the other women.

Grace Scribner (1882-1922) attended Chicago Training School from
1905-07, entering the year she turned 23. She grew up in lumber camps
with limited opportunities for an education, and as a teenager, decided
to become a missionary. In 1908 she began to work with Isabelle Horton as a part time editorial assistant for the *Deaconess Advocate.* She used
her stenographic skills working for the *Epworth Herald,* a publication
for Methodist youth and young adult work.[102] Scribner was a member
of the Stenographer's Union and belonged to the Women's Trade Union
League, which Mary McDowell had helped to found. She was a reflective person and a talented writer.

In 1912, the Federation took a big step when it decided to hire staff.
It engaged Harry Ward to direct the work of MFSS. Between January
and March he addressed church groups, Epworth Leagues, and attended

---

101. Records for Bertha Fowler do not show how long she participated. McDowell
and Horton were signing a 1911 peace statement for the Federation, writing, and chairing
committees or regions up through 1914.

102. Grace Scribner, *An American Pilgrimage,* ed. by Winifred L. Chappell (New York,
NY: Vanguard Press, 1927) xxiii. See also Miriam Crist, "A Story of Two Women: Grace
Scribner and Winifred Chappell," New York, NY: Union Theological Seminary, unpublished
paper, 1979, 3.

18 conferences. He visited Oregon, Washington, California, Montana, Idaho, Colorado, Illinois, Indiana, and Pennsylvania. Ward spoke at 118 meetings in two months gathering attention far and wide for the cause of social service. The funds he raised enabled the organization to employ as a full-time office secretary Grace Scribner, who had been working for the Methodist young adult publication, *Epworth Herald,* as well as the *Deaconess Advocate.* Ward gained wide recognition for his abilities.

When Scribner took a position in Evanston as full time office manager and secretary for the Methodist Federation for Social Service in 1913, she worked directly with Harry Ward shortly after he started his new position as executive secretary of the Federation. He was pastor at Euclid Avenue Methodist Episcopal Church in Oak Park, about half an hour by trolley from the new commodious home of the Chicago Training School. Scribner applied herself to editing, publishing, and running the office of the Federation.

In 1914, Ward joined the faculty of Boston University School of Theology as its first professor of Social Service.[103] Since the office of the Methodist Federation also moved to Boston to be where he was, this meant Grace Scribner also made the move along with her job. From her new office she continued to assist Josiah Meyer, husband of Lucy Rider Meyer, with publishing the *Deaconess Advocate.*

In 1918, Scribner moved again as the Federation office followed Ward to New York where he took a faculty position at Union Theological Seminary. Scribner's new title was assistant secretary of the Federation. She became joint editor of the *Social Service Bulletin.*

As a person who struggled with inner conflicts and emotions, Scribner went through a profound period in her life as a young adult when she deconstructed all the social institutions in her life. She started by attacking her own religious beliefs and taking them apart. She turned her criticism on economic concepts, sex, and every aspect of life. As she sought the truth, everything crumbled. In the long run, she believed fervently in the future of human beings and in humankind that is yet to be.[104]

In reflective letters, Grace Scribner described her commitment to

---

103. Eugene Link, *Labor-Religion Prophet: The Times and Life of Harry F. Ward,* (Boulder, CO: Westview Press, 1984) 56.

104. Chappell, Winifred, ed. *"An American Pilgrimage: Portions of the Letters of Grace Scribner,"* (New York, NY: Vanguard Press, 1927) 82.

making responsible ethical choices. She noticed the way one person has an impact on others. She held this belief:

> That I have no right, whatever my personal convictions may be, to endanger the work or life of another—and that that must be avoided at any cost to myself. The war taught that bitter lesson—that one cannot follow one's personal convictions without counting the cost to others.[105]

In 1922, a careless driver tragically killed Grace Scribner. Winifred Chappell inherited her books, her typewriter, and her job.

Winifred Chappell (1879-1951) graduated from Northwestern University with a B.A. in Philosophy in 1903. Like Fowler, Chappell taught public school for three years before attending Chicago Training School from 1906-07. She was consecrated deaconess by the Rock River Conference of the Methodist Episcopal Church. She taught Bible and Greek at the Chicago Training School in 1907 and continued while attending the Divinity School of the University of Chicago in 1909.[106] While in seminary she was influenced by George Albert Coe, of the Boston personalism school of thought, who was teaching philosophy at Northwestern. It was unusual for Chappell, as a woman, to attend theological school, just as it had been for Fowler, and she would have experienced gender discrimination. Chappell served as Assistant Principal of the Chicago Training School for five years, and in 1913 also taught courses in Social Service and New Testament.[107]

Following Scribner's death in 1922, Chappell worked as research secretary for the Methodist Federation, preparing material for the bimonthly *Social Service Bulletin*. Chappell was a founding member of the Fellowship of Socialist Christians. She joined the Federation for a New Social Order (1920-21) and belonged to the League for Industrial

---

105. *Ibid.*, 87.

106. Miriam Crist, "Winifred Chappell: 'Everybody on the Left Knew Her,'" *Radical Religion*, 5:1, 1980, 22. See also Miriam Crist, "Winifred L. Chappell: Everybody on the Left Knew Her," *Women in New Worlds* ed. Hilah F. Thomas and Rosemary Skinner Keller (Nashville: Abingdon, 1981) 362-78 and Isabelle Horton, *The Builders, A Story of Faith and Works* (Chicago: Belle L. James, 1910) 213.

107. Letter from Winifred Chappell to Lucy Rider Meyer published in Isabelle Horton, *High Adventure: The Life of Lucy Rider Meyer*, (New York, NY: The Methodist Book Concern, 1929) 212.

Democracy.[108] She served on the Federal Council of Churches and the YWCA (Young Women's Christian Association) Industrial Committee.[109] Chappell specialized in labor struggles of women in industry. In the 1920s she knew what was going on in the frequent strikes and in the steel, coal, and textile industries. Chappell wrote for *The Christian Century* and was a popular speaker on the lecture circuit.[110] In 1936 she was hired by Claude Williams, a southern labor activist from the People's Institute of Applied Religion. She went with Williams to Detroit to work on labor issues and eventually returned to Chicago where she died in 1951.

The years 1912 and 1913 were a turning point in the life of the Federation. Progressive views similar to those of the Federation echoed in American party politics. The Federation's work influenced the 1912 General Conference. Policies adopted by the conference reflected some of the Federation's concerns. Changes were taking place in the culture. The Federation clarified and expanded its work. The deaconess movement touched the lives of hundreds of thousands. As it responded to immigration and widespread poverty, the Methodist Episcopal Church was beginning to develop a prophetic identity that spoke to institutions and responded to social needs. The church began to understand salvation in a broader way.

Social problems were massive. The Methodist Federation for Social Service had been born in a financial panic in 1907.[111] The panic was followed by widespread unemployment in 1908 that prompted MFSS to publish their first pamphlet, "Our Immediate Program."[112] Millions of Americans were so destitute that both Republicans and Democrats campaigned for change. William Taft, a Republican, was elected President. He worked against corporate trusts and combinations that restrained freedom of trade. By 1912, talking about and working for social improvement was popular. Woodrow Wilson, a Democrat, was

108. Crist, "A Story of Two Women: Grace Scribner and Winifred Chappell," 12, 14, 15. Crist, "Winifred Chappell," *Radical Religion* 5:1, 1980, 22.

109. Ibid., 23.

110. Winifred Chappell's speaking tours included a visit to my mother's home church, Sellwood Methodist Church, in Portland, Oregon, and being a keynote speaker for the Epworth League Institute at Falls City, Oregon, about 1936.

111. Huber, *"History,"* 116.

112. Methodist Federation for Social Service, "Our Immediate Program," (Chicago: 1908).

elected President. He capitalized on a progressive spirit sweeping the nation. Mary McDowell had worked on labor issues with Eugene Debs, Socialist party candidate for President, who tallied over a million votes. Debs thought that the profit motive and capitalism were undermining the social order.[113] Economic instability continued to plague the country. Living conditions grew worse each year until 1916 when the war in Europe began to stimulate the American economy.[114]

Federation leaders were changing their thinking and beginning to have an influence on others. MFSS came to the 1912 General Conference well prepared to respond to four questions asked by the General Conference in 1908:

1. What principles and measurements of social reform are worthy of support by the church?
2. How should church agencies be used in promoting such principles and measures?
3. What can best be accomplished through cooperation with other denominations?
4. How can the church adapt courses of study to make preachers more efficient in social reform?[115]

Their response formed the basis of a new resolution, "The Church and Social Problems," adopted by the General Conference and placed in the 1912 *Discipline*.[116] The resolution developed platform statements on the role of the church, ministers and laity, theological schools, and other church related organizations in dealing with social problems. For the first time the Episcopal Address (a State of the Church speech), included a clear indictment of "organized capital," reflecting a changing sentiment in the denomination. The bishops were concerned about corporate conspiracies that raised prices for the poor. The Episcopal Address linked corporate influence in government with policies that usurped the rights of the poor. The church also expressed concern that labor unions were jeopardizing the rights of non-union laborers.

---

113. Upton "Sinclair, *The Jungle*, (New York: The Viking Press, 1947) viii.

114. *Ibid.*, 117.

115. These questions are paraphrased from the *Social Service Bulletin*, 2:1, January 1912, 2.

116. The Methodist Episcopal Church, *Discipline*, 1912, (Cincinnati: The Methodist Book Concern, 1912), Para. 564.

As Methodists have done for a long time, the 1912 General Conference adopted statements that included both liberal and conservative opinions on the same topic.

The Church and Social Problems

We live in an age in which the vast enterprises essential to the progress of the world require the association of men of large means under corporate management. Out of this necessity have grown serious wrongs and consequent resistance.

Organized capital stands indicted at the bar of public judgment for the gravest crimes against the common welfare. Among the counts in that indictment are such as these: 1. Conspiring to advance prices on the staple commodities indispensable to the life, well-being, and progress of all the people. 2. Resorting to adulteration of foods, fabrics and materials in order to increase profits already excessive. 3. Destroying the competition in trade through which relief might be expected under normal conditions. 4. Suborning [creating wrongful] legislation and thus robbing the people of the first orderly recourse of the weak against the strong.

These are sins against humanity. If God hates any sin above another, it must be the robbery of the poor and defenseless. Otherwise his love fails when it is most needed and might find its largest opportunity. There is no betrayal more base than that which uses the hospitality of the house to plunder its inmates, unless it be that form of treason which so perverts the purpose and machinery of popular government as to turn its power against the people who trust and support it.[117]

With this resolution, the church made a prophetic statement. It claimed a theology that believes that God takes the side of the poor and defenseless. The idea that a nation would be a beacon of hope for refugees and immigrants and plunder them and their labor for the enrichment of the wealthy they declared to be a betrayal of hospitality

---

117. *Deaconess Advocate*, 29:7, July 1912, 9.

and Christian faith. The prophetic voice of the church identified one problem after another. It set a high standard, encouraging members to right these wrongs. Words need to be followed by actions, but words also help to inspire actions. A generation of MFSS leaders have motivated and inspired church members, as people of faith, to take action with social service, advocating in the political arena.

During the years 1912 and 1913, the *Deaconess Advocate* hoped to inspire action when it introduced a new page called "Social Service." Signed feature articles provided more thorough treatment of social issues than in the past. The articles made connections between major social problems and pressed for more long range solutions involving complex treatment of social issues. During this period, key persons that this book has examined were all publishing articles in this magazine.

In 1912, Winifred Chappell wrote a series of seven articles about social service. She pressed readers to take social questions beyond common solutions being generally discussed. She added a holistic approach and looked for the roots of the problems. Deaconesses had stumbled on a complex set of interrelated issues. In January 1912, she wrote,

> The church builds hospitals; why should she [the deaconess] not concern herself with the prevention of disease?...She consistently holds to her belief in the dignity of labor; why not make the conditions of labor tolerable? Unwittingly, the deaconess has encountered a galaxy of twentieth century problems—bad housing, work accidents, infant mortality, child labor, child delinquency.[118]

Chappell declared that a community support system nurtured by "whole-souled support of the Christian church" offers hope for a solution.[119] Chappell made clear her belief that the relation of the individual to society is such that:

> the salvation of the one without the other is impossible, and that it is her [the deaconess'] God-appointed task to help the

---

118. Winifred Chappell, "The Deaconess and Social Service," *Deaconess Advocate* 27:1, January 1912, 7.
119. *Ibid,*7.

church so to cooperate with social service agencies in the divine work of perfecting society that every man [sic] born into the world may have a chance to live and to live "abundantly."[120]

As the series continued, Chappell addressed problems of overlapping organized relief, public health, and working women. Chappell believed that working women, though busy and exhausted, have a wealth of first-hand information on working conditions. Working women have a responsibility to cooperate with churchwomen so that they could aid working women to improve their condition. Together women could change working conditions for women across the board.

> [The help] may be better laws, or pressure on the legislature to pass pending legislation; it may be homes for working women, or classes in sewing, cooking, language or art; it may be opportunity for clean recreation; perhaps the supreme need will be for a friend.[121]

Building positive relationships between people can increase the sense of care and reciprocity. When connections are built, people can see the need for laws that will help those they care about.

In March 1913, Grace Scribner wrote a column for the *Deaconess Advocate* on "The Business Woman's Contribution to Community Service." She referred to "unusual competition with men in business and the professions" based on "the common belief that single women, 'having no one but themselves to look after' may assume responsibilities which no married daughter or son would be expected to assume." The same expectations were not held for single men. She urged women to take "an interest in the work of other women, especially women in the factories and shops...."[122]

In September and November, 1913, Mary McDowell's articles about the Slovakian-American wedding reception in the saloon and

---

120. Winifred Chappell, "The Deaconess and the Resources of the Community," *Deaconess Advocate*, 27:2, February 1912, 9.

121. Winifred Chappell, "The Deaconess and the Working Woman," *Deaconess Advocate* 27:5, May 1912, 9.

122. Grace Scribner, "The Business Woman's Contribution to Community Service," *Deaconess Advocate*, 28:3, March 1913, 9.

about "Thanksgiving in Packingtown" were published in the *Deaconess Advocate,* completing the appearance of articles by four key Methodist Federation women and by Harry Ward in the same publication in the space of two years.

Between 1907 and 1914, learning from the thinking and experience of these emerging female practical theologians, the Methodist Federation for Social Service found its voice, calling the nation to live by a higher moral standard of respect for its citizens. MFSS provided organizational leadership and formative ethical language that helped persuade a nation to raise the quality of life for its citizens.

Over the next three decades, MFSS helped bring about major changes in government and society. MFSS was well connected with the cluster of organizations that lobbied for and won major protections and benefits for American families. These included the forty-hour work week, the right to organize labor, child labor laws, Social Security, Workers' Compensation, food supplement programs, price supports for farmers, tenant rights, safety standards in industry, and food and drug regulations. Women played an integral part in making these changes.

Deaconesses continued to help address social problems, but new doors were opening for women to expand their education, enter teaching and nursing professions, and earn a living which changed the appeal of the low-paying vocation of deaconess. Women began to look for more diversity in their career paths. The deaconess movement peaked during these years.

In 1914, MFSS began to introduce social service and the Christian concept of radical egalitarianism that would characterize the hoped-for new social order into the curricula of the church. For several years, Ward had written articles that were published in a dozen church magazines. The new program was more specific. Ward wrote weekly articles, and Scribner wrote monthly articles plus occasional articles for numerous other publications. Winifred Chappell published one of Scribner's pieces as a pamphlet called "Social Service for Church Women." After Scribner's tragic death, Chappell published her biography, *An American Pilgrimage: Portions of the Letters of Grace Scribner.*

Harry Ward envisioned a special role for women in social service. Just as women leaders such as Frances Willard, Lucy Rider Meyer, and Belle Horton had done, he claimed that the gospel called for expanding the place of women in contemporary life. He thought that women should use their ability to be nurturers. He expected that the majority of social workers should be women, and that most of them would come from churches. He stated, "Church women have a large part to play in spreading the leaven which is to transform our present human society into the ideal social order proclaimed by Jesus." The role he saw for women was to "simplify our complex social relationships, to soften hardness" and to remove injustice by sharing in the community the "spirit and character of the family and home." He believed that women helped men to better understand that life is not all about business. Women also could help people measure the worth of life in terms of what it means to be human.[123] Women's tenderness and ability to be more in touch with emotions than men would advance the cause of justice.

Coming from a generation that grew up believing in the domestic role of women in the family and the life of the nation, Ward was a man of his times in the way he described the different roles of men and women. Even in his later years, Ward never did accept the leadership of women in the same way he accepted men. Because he was more satisfied working with women who deferred to his leadership, he felt closer to Grace Scribner than he did to Winifred Chappell. When she worked for the Federation, Chappell was a more popular speaker than Ward. His feelings about this may have prevented him from having as close a relationship with Chappell, who was perceived by some as being keener than Ward. Some women who had working relationships with Ward later in his life would even say that he was dictatorial.[124]

In those years when women in the United States did not have the right to vote, gradually the role of women in the Methodist Federation and the church changed. In 1908 the Methodist Episcopal Church, under pressure from the deaconess movement, women's organizations, and the broadening social opportunities for women, began to open the door for women to hold leadership positions in the local church. The Judicial Council decided that "the pronouns *he, his,* and *him,* when used in the *Discipline* with reference to Stewards, Class Leaders, and

---

123. Harry F. Ward, "The Church Woman and Social Service," *Deaconess Advocate*, 27:11, November 1912, 9.

124. Alice G. Knotts, Interview with Dorothy McConnell, May 10, 1984. McConnell was Associate General Secretary of the Woman's Division of the Board of Missions of The Methodist Church, 1964-1968. Alice G. Knotts, Interview with Thelma Stevens, December 7-8, 1983. Thelma Stevens was Executive Secretary of Christian Social Relations for the Woman's Division of the Board of Missions of The Methodist Church from 1940-68.

Sunday School Superintendents, shall not be so construed as to exclude women from such offices."[125] At last women were given the blessing and official recognition of their leadership in the local church.

MFSS was unusual in being inclusive of women in leadership. In the Methodist Episcopal Church women held no national leadership roles unless they were part of a gender-segregated organization such as the Woman's Foreign Missionary Society, the Woman's Home Missionary Society, or the deaconess movement. MFSS treated women leaders as models for extending the home sphere. Women joined the Federation, growing the ranks of women who engaged in social service.[126] They contributed generously to the Federation with their time and effort.

The *Social Service Bulletin* ran a series of stories about the ways various members were promoting social service. It noted, "Isabelle Horton of the Deaconess Institute, St. Louis, has been giving studies in Christian Social Service at Epworth League institutes."[127] Winifred Chappell was reportedly making inquiry into the social service activities of deaconesses.[128] The publication recommended a book by Isabelle Horton, *What Happened to Ted.*[129]

The Federation developed a Speaker's Bureau list of 100 speakers. They were listed by name, topic, and address where they could be reached. One woman appeared on the list with ninety-nine men. Mary McDowell was available to speak on "The Helpless in Industry" or on women's suffrage. A month later, Winifred Chappell's name appeared with thirteen additional men's names. Chappell was prepared to speak on "The Spiritual Significance of the Woman Movement," "Christian Women and the Social Evil," and "The Church and the New Social Conscience."

This account of the role of women in developing social gospel awareness and providing leadership in the formative years of the Methodist Federation for Social Service concludes with the story of a vote. The Federation published a ballot in the November 1914 issue of the

125. *The Discipline*, 1908, Par. 40, 464.
126. The *Social Service Bulletin* reported that Burdette Brown served as secretary of the Methodist Child Welfare Society of MFSS. In November 1914, Miss E. Jean Oram of Cleveland was elected to the Executive Committee. SSB February 1913, November 1914.
127. *Social Service Bulletin*, 2:6, November 1912, 3. The Epworth League was an organization of Methodist youth and young adults ranging in age from 13 to 30.
128. *Social Service Bulletin,* 3:4, January 1913, 3.
129. *Social Service Bulletin,* 3:4, July 1913.

Social Service Bulletin. Members of the Federation were asked to decide whether or not to increase from nine to eleven the number of persons serving on the Executive Committee of the Federation in order to add two women. The members adopted this proposal, giving women a stronger position in the leadership of the Federation.[130]

The following year, the work of the Federation was reorganized regionally. Isabelle Horton was recognized as a leader in the eastern group. Mary McDowell and Winifred Chappell were members of the executive committee of the western group. Women entered the inner circle of leadership in the Methodist Federation.

A key step to breaking down a system of social inequities is that of accepting women in leadership. The Federation took this important step. Mary McDowell, Isabelle Horton, Bertha Fowler, Grace Scribner, and Winifred Chappell went the extra mile by doing their job and breaking the tradition of gender inequality at the same time.

Years passed. The Methodist Federation stood up against giants during the U.S. Steel strikes. Harry Ward and the Federation helped organize the ACLU in the 1930s to defend civil liberties. The dream years of a new social order didn't arrive.

Power and wealth are strong forces that stand up against a new social order not based on profit. Over the course of a century, the Methodist Federation was attacked from the religious and political right for its agenda and desire to bring in a new egalitarian social order. The Methodist Federation for Social Action (re-named in 1945) gleaned ideas from Socialists and Communists about how to provide more equitably for people regardless of class or difference. MFSA passed through dark years, advocating for the right of every citizen of the U.S. to choose his or her own political affiliation. Because anything Communist was nicknamed "red," critics labeled MFSA "pink" for associating with Communists. Certain conservative Methodists who wanted to discredit the Federation made alliances with J. Edgar Hoover of the FBI and started files on MFSA leaders. From 1952-54, people spread lies and innuendos about the organization. MFSA leaders were followed by the

---

130. No record shows who was elected. Mary McDowell had chaired a committee and served on the executive committee following the 1908 meeting. Since Isabelle Horton took leadership on the executive committee in the eastern group and Winifred Chappell served with the western group, they may have been the women elected to serve on the executive committee, joining Mary McDowell.

CHAPTER 8

FBI and called on by Congress to defend themselves before the House Committee on Un-American Activities. This colorful past was part of the harassment of the Federation for siding with people who were critical of social systems that entrenched or increased poverty. More recently MFSA advocated for civil rights, women's rights, and the rights of gay men and lesbian women. To this day, in the halls of Capitol Hill and General Conferences, the struggles continue.

STUDY QUESTIONS

1. Have you ever experienced a turning point in your life when you made a commitment to do (or not to do) something for the rest of your life? What brought you to this point?
2. Have you ever belonged to a church or organization that went through a time of rapid change? Describe what this was like. Are there any reasons to do this again?
3. Name one principle and one social reform that is worthy of support by the church.
4. Have you encountered gender expectations in the church? In society? Describe. how they have affected you and your family.
5. The author claims: "A key step to breaking down a system of social inequities is that of accepting women in leadership." Do you agree?
6. Do you think that discrimination occurs when people think about the world in dualistic categories such as male/female or rich/poor? What are the roots of discrimination? What could be done differently?

A woman demonstrates doing laundry.

REFLECTIONS ON LIVING OUT JUSTICE

T HE WOMEN WHO gave years of service to the Methodist Federation for Social Service were passionate about their commitments. Their deaconess work and membership in the Federation provided an opportunity to live out their faith, to make a difference for many people. To help make a better world, they worked to reverse social values that supported a corrupt and unjust social order.

They looked to Jesus to understand the change in attitudes needed to reverse the prevailing social order. In Jesus' time, people expected that religious leaders should be honored, that wealthy men should be respected, that poor people lived lives that fell short of God's commandments, and that ordinary people should offer charity to the poor. Many religious leaders taught that happiness was grounded in strictly following religious law.

In contrast, these Christian women 1900 years later read the Bible and came to believe that many people lived in poverty not because their lives inadequately glorified God but because social systems did not offer them an equal opportunity in life. They were denied opportunities for education, employed at low wages, sustained by inadequate diets, and exposed to illness and injury. These Christian women knew that Jesus had reached out to social outcasts and displaced persons such as lepers, mentally ill persons, chronically ill and crippled persons, a hemorrhaging woman, foreigners, refugees, widows, and unmarried women with lovers. They read from Isaiah the foretelling of a messiah who would right wrongs by bringing about a new social order. Some knew by heart the prayer of Mary, who dedicated her son, Jesus, to God that he might bring in justice for a God who claimed that oppressors would be brought down by being immersed in their own conceit.

These Christian women knew that Jesus overturned social expectations. He described a heavenly banquet at which those rustled in from the streets at the last minute were seated in places of honor. He touched lepers and healed the blind. He forgave people who were crippled by guilt, although religious leaders said he was doing what only God could do. By interacting with the poor he snubbed people deemed important on account of their wealth. He overturned the tables of a big racket that soaked the poor at the temple in Jerusalem. When criticized for these actions, Jesus did not conform, but continued to preach the message of God's love for all people. His persistence, of course, led those in power who felt threatened by his unusual and counter-cultural actions to take Jesus through a mock court that ordered his execution on the grounds that he was a threat to the nation. After Jesus' death, the disciples realized that they had experienced God's love when they were with Jesus. At last they understood the power of God whose hatred of injustice and love for people would never end.

This is the grand gospel that grew from acorn to oak tree in five Methodist women who focused their whole lives around being disciples of Jesus. They had a passion for justice and believed that they could help people by overcoming the ills of society. They stood against evil and believed that the whole family of God deserved to be treated with respect.

While much Christian preaching and teaching had focused on the change that God works in the life of an individual, the Methodist Federation focused on the responsibility of Christians to stand up for justice and to be in mission, reaching out to others with long term solutions to huge problems. They believed that Jesus preached good news of the dignity and worth of all persons. To them, the most effective means to reach out was to organize. Then, when organizing failed to bring about the quality of life and society that they envisioned, they began to critique the foundations of the social system that trapped whole classes of people in poverty and they began to conceive possible new foundations for society.

Any generation that doesn't know its history is prone to repeat the failures of human nature. The culture of the United States is becoming increasingly materialistic. The market is god. The need for resources, labor, and markets drives politics, policies, and wars. Where the market is god, politicians are bought, wars enrich the wealthy, and poor people pay the most taxes and suffer in poverty. The "isms" of gender, race, nationality, and economic class are maintained to service the market.

The context of mission and ministry that cried out for Christian leadership one hundred years ago still cries out today. Economic conditions insult the claim of the Declaration of Independence that all persons are created equal. Massive efforts to focus the attention of the nation on caring for its people have been diverted. In the heart of communities of thousands or millions where people are surrounded by humanity, people can feel lonely, disconnected, and isolated.

Poverty is still a huge problem. As of 2005, the official poverty rate in the U.S. was 12.6%. Among children under the age of 18 the rate climbed to 17.6%. The 2006 qualifying income for one person under age 65 to be described as living in poverty was $10,488 per year. Over a ten year period, approximately 40% of persons living in the U.S. lived in poverty for a period of time. In 2004, more than 15% or 45.8 million Americans in the U.S. had no health insurance.[131] The per capita income in the U.S. ranks 19th among nations in the world, and neighboring Mexico has dropped from 22nd to 79th in per capita income over the past century. In Mexico, 40% of the population falls below Mexican guidelines for poverty level. No wonder there is a large wave of new immigrants coming from Mexico, often arriving with no more than they can carry. They come with a dream of starting a new life that offers hope. Too often, the dream of escaping poverty eludes them.

Yet the dream lives. God calls Christians to be concerned when the names and faces of the poor have changed but the problems remain. Christians today can call for the U.S. to re-examine the founding principles of its social systems. Christians can help the nation reshape the teachings that create hierarchies of race, gender, national origin, and class.

Immigrants to the U.S. opened a door that helped a group of dedicated Christian women grow their faith. The Hebrew scripture taught people to provide hospitality to strangers and sojourners. The condi-

---

131. www.usgovinfo.about.com. February 10, 2007.

tions under which immigrants lived then and still live today have shown both the church and the nation where social problems are located and what it takes to fix them. They teach Christians where God calls them to grow their faith.

The faith and understanding of the gospel of Jesus grew in the women who gave leadership to the Methodist Federation for Social Service. When people were hurting and suffering in their daily lives, these women felt called to do more than give a handout. They wanted to change the whole social system so that power was shared and workers could enjoy the benefits of their own labor. They dreamed of a society in which people who were unable to work would still be able to live with dignity. They did not dream of imposing their faith on others but of sharing respect for all persons. They could not, with integrity, separate politics from the values their faith had taught them.

Women who belonged to MFSS helped to lay the groundwork for the development of social gospel radicalism that emerged after World War I. First, they made a commitment to persons. They valued human life and wanted people to be treated with dignity and respect, regardless of race, nationality, gender, or economic class. Their emphasis on God's love for persons was in conflict with the profit motive of industry and the poverty of the cities. They recognized that industry and corporations make decisions for their own benefit, such as dismissing workers, or paying minimum wages.

Second, they recognized that people living in human communities are interdependent. The whole system contributes to what happens to individuals in that system. The condition of an individual has an impact on the community. Observing this interdependency provided information essential to the intellectual development of a critique of social systems.

Third, the emphasis on scholarly Bible study, the study of social science and social service prepared women to think creatively, to doubt constructively, to understand justice issues, and to use their best intellectual skills to approach problems. Graduate education of women contributed to the development of social reconstruction views among early MFSS founders. It led them to challenge power brokers.

Fourth, women in MFSS learned from human misery that they encountered in the inner city. As they probed for the causes, they critiqued the "isms" which were the pillars for the foundation of capitalism—classism, racism, sexism. All of these emphasized differences that were used to establish winners and losers in society. There were gender differences in the approach of men and women to the theme of social service. Men tended to take an intellectual approach to the study of social problems. Women learned from their experiences, their contact with the poor and their friends who were working with the poor. Jane Addams observed, "...If you study almost any of the great reform movements you will find that they started, not with people who theorized about civic problems, but with those who came into daily contact with the poor."[132]

Fifth, the women in MFSS raised important questions about the inadequacies of the social engineering approach to social problems that failed to get to the roots of problems. Though McDowell succeeded in establishing garbage collection services for Packingtown, it took fifteen years of hard lobbying, massive investigations, and countless deaths. She must have wondered why the price was so high, whether anything would change, and if so, when. She found that industrial leaders were ignorant about problems in industry, but that after they were informed, slight changes were made but problems continued.

Isabelle Horton began to doubt that the church could save the masses. She turned for help to a coalition of community sources. When people in the cities still were hardly any better off, she must have wondered why. She wrote and taught, hoping to attract young women to the task of social betterment. She began to envision a new social order.

Winifred Chappell suggested that since the church could build hospitals, it should direct its attention also to the prevention of disease. The church believed in the dignity of labor, so "why not make the conditions of labor tolerable?"[133] She was ready to look deeper than the obvious at a time when there was no public consensus about why America's social problems were so vast.

The stage was set. Women leaders in MFSS helped uncover the inadequacies of social engineering and helped the organization commit to build a new social order. The task of analysis of the larger social system lay ahead.

The Methodist Federation was poised to side with workers

---

132. Jane Addams, "Commencement Address," *Deaconess Advocate*, 22:6, June 1906, 9.

133. Winifred Chappell, "The Deaconess and Social Service," *Deaconess Advocate*, 27:1, January 1912, 7.

in national labor disputes, advocate for children's welfare, for the government to form a Food and Drug Administration, and for Social Security. The Federation became an advocate for human rights, women's rights, and the rights of all persons regardless of ethnicity, race, or sexual orientation.

Today the Methodist Federation for Social Action continues its work with 38 chapters in the U.S. MFSA relocated its office from New York to Washington, D.C. There is plenty of work still to be done. In the U.S. there is no constitutional amendment protecting the rights of women. Considering that unequal treatment of women or any person is at the root of a dysfunctional society, this needs attention. The lessons that these women learned about working for justice will be pivotal to the critical problems of global warming. Peoples of the world will need to unite to address planetary issues. Every plan that creates winners and losers will add to the losses of the entire planet.

As these women discovered, doing justice requires sharing. Living out justice is about the sharing of knowledge and power. This turns upside down the way social institutions usually operate when they gather power to themselves. If thousands of non-profit organizations that give people tools and skills for self-empowerment were to rise up and encourage voters to elect officials to seats in government with the intent of giving power to the people, we would see a new social order. It would make a difference if we could have fair elections. There is no time to waste. Our culture can learn from the experience of these Methodist women and the Methodist Federation about the strength of gathering together resources to solve problems. Committed people can change the attitudes and commitments of a nation so that it cares for its people.

Margaret Mead said, "Never doubt that a small group of thoughtful committed persons can change the world; indeed, it's the only thing that ever has."[134] When people care that their social institutions—schools, organizations, corporations, and governments—are compassionate and kind, just and impartial, they lift up hope and live out justice. The whole world becomes a place where God's love reigns.

---

134. www.brinyquote.com/quotes/authors/m/margaret_mead.html.

CHAPTER 9

STUDY QUESTIONS

1. Of the things Jesus taught and did, what most inspires you?
2. The author writes, "Any generation that doesn't know its history is prone to repeat the failures of human nature." Give some examples of failures that repeat.
3. Do you believe that there can be social changes? Why or why not?
4. Jane Addams said, "If you study almost any of the great reform movements you will find that they started, not with people who theorized about civic problems, but with those who came into daily contact with the poor." What evidence would you cite to support this claim?
5. The author claims, "Peoples of the world will need to unite to address planetary issues. Every plan that creates winners and losers will add to the losses of the entire planet." Which response is closest to your perspective?
    a) We need competition. Competition is an incentive.
    b) Some people are lazy. There is no way to get everyone's cooperation.
    c) Everyone can do something. Every drop of water adds to the ocean.
    d) The Bible says that if one part of the body suffers, the whole body suffers.
    e) Other. Describe.
6. The author concludes, "When people care that their social institutions…are compassionate and kind, just and impartial, they lift up hope and live out justice. The whole world becomes a place where God's love reigns." What commitment do you make to lift up hope and live out justice?

Winifred Chappell, 1917.

BIBLIOGRAPHY

Addams, Jane, "Commencement Address." *Deaconess Advocate*, 22:6. June, 1906.

Altschuler, Glenn, C. "Walter Rauschenbusch's Theology: The Church and the Social Gospel," *Foundation,* April-June, 1979.

Balch, William M. "The Pulpit as a Social Force." Worth M. Tippy, ed. *The Socialized Church.* New York, NY: Eaton & Mains, 1909.

Chappell, Winifred, ed. *"An American Pilgrimage: Portions of the Letters of Grace Scribner."* New York, NY: Vanguard Press, 1927.

————. "The Deaconess and Social Service." *Deaconess Advocate,* 27:1. January, 1912.

Crist, Miriam, "A Story of Two Women: Grace Scribner and Winifred Chappell," New York, NY: Union Theological Seminary, unpublished paper, 1979.

————. "Winifred Chappell: Everyone on the Left Knew Her." *Radical Religion.* 5:1, 1980.

Deaconess Advocate. Chicago, IL. 1894-1914.

Dougherty, Mary Agness. "The Methodist Deaconess, 1885-1918: A Study in Religious Feminism." Davis, CA: University of California, 1979. Ph. D. Dissertation.

Edwards, Wendy J. Deichmann and Carolyn DeSwarte Gifford, eds. Gender and the Social Gospel. Chicago, IL: University of Illinois Press, 2003.

Fowler, Bertha. "The Deaconess as the Pastor's Social Assistant." Worth M. Tippy, ed. The Socialized Church. New York, NY: Eaton & Mains, 1909.

Gorrell, Donald K. "The Methodist Federation for Social Service and the Social Creed." Methodist History, 13:2, 1975.

Horton, Isabelle. High Adventure, The Life of Lucy Rider Meyer. New York, NY: The Methodist Book Concern, 1929.

———. The Burden of the City. New York, NY: Fleming H. Revell Company, 1904.

———. "The Deaconess in Social Settlement Work." Worth M. Tippy, ed. The Socialized Church. New York, NY: Eaton & Mains, 1909.

———. "The Deaconess and Social Service." Deaconess Advocate 27:1, January, 1912.

———. "The Deaconess and the Resources of the Community." Deaconess Advocate. 27:2. February, 1912.

———. "The Deaconess and the Working Woman." Deaconess Advocate. 27:5. May, 1912.

Huber, John Milton. "A History of the Federation for Social Action." Boston University, Ph. D Thesis, 1949.

Jones, Maldwyn Allen. American Immigration. Chicago, University of Chicago Press, 1960.

King, William McGuire. *The Emergence of Social Gospel Radicalism in American Methodism.* Cambridge, MA: Harvard University, 1977. Unpublished dissertation.

———. "The Emergence of Social Gospel Radicalism: The Methodist Case." *Church History.* December 1981.

Knepper, Jeanne Gayle. *"Thy Kingdom Come: The Methodist Federation for Social Service and Human Rights."* Ph. D. Dissertation, The Iliff School of Theology, 1996.

Knotts, Alice G. Interview with Dorothy McConnell, May 10, 1984.

———. Interview with Thelma Stevens, December 7-8, 1983.

———. *Fellowship of Love: Methodist Women Changing American Racial Attitudes, 1920-1968.* Nashville, TN: Kingswood Press, 1996.

———. "Women Founders of the Methodist Federation for Social Service." Unpublished paper. 1984.

Link, Eugene. *Labor-Religion Prophet: The Times and Life of Harry F. Ward.* Boulder, CO: Westview Press, 1984.

McClain, George D. "Pioneering Social Gospel Radicalism, An Overview of the History of the Methodist Federation for Social Action," *Radical Religion* 5:1, 1980.

———. "The History of 'The Social Creed.'" www.liberalslikechrist. org Accessed 18 March 2007.

McDowell, Mary. "The Social Assistant." Worth M. Tippy, ed. *The Socialized Church.*

Methodist Episcopal Church. *Discipline.* Cincinnati: The Methodist Book Concern, 1908, 1912.

"Our Immediate Program." Chicago, IL: Methodist Federation for Social Service. 1908.

Rossinow, Doug. "The Radicalization of the Social Gospel: Harry F. Ward and the Search for a New Social Order, 1898-1936." *Religion and American Culture,* 15:1. Winter, 2005.

Scribner, Grace. "The Business Woman's Contribution to Community Service." *Deaconess Advocate,* 28:3. March, 1913.

Sinclair, Upton. *The Jungle.* New York, NY: The Viking Press, 1947.

"Social Service." Chicago, IL: Methodist Federation for Social Service, 1908.

Social Service Bulletin. Chicago, IL: Methodist Federation for Social Service, 1908-1914.

Tippy, Worth M. "The Organization of a Church for Social Ministry." Harry F. Ward, ed. *Social Ministry.* New York, NY: Eaton & Mains, 1910.

Tippy, Worth M. ed. *The Socialized Church.* New York, NY: Eaton & Mains, 1909.

Ward, Harry F. "The Church Woman and Social Service." *Deaconess Advocate* 27:11, November, 1912.

————. "The Labor Movement." Harry F. Ward, ed. *Social Ministry,* New York, NY: Eaton & Mains, 1910.

————. ed. *Social Ministry.* New York, NY: Eaton & Mains, 1910.

Welch, Herbert, "The Church and the Social Need." Worth M. Tippy. *The Socialized Church.* New York, NY: Eaton & Mains, 1909.

White, Ronald C., Jr. and C. Howard Hopkins, *The Social Gospel: Religion and Reform in Changing America.* Philadelphia: Temple University Press, 1976.

Wilson, Howard E. *Mary McDowell, Neighbor.* Chicago, IL: University of Chicago Press, 1928.

INDEX

F

FBI 82, 83
Federal Council of Churches 61, 74
food 10, 13, 15, 17, 28, 39, 40, 41,
    42, 48, 49, 69, 79
Fowler, Bertha v, vii, 1, 9, 10, 33, 41,
    45, 46, 47, 48, 49, 50, 51, 66,
    68, 71, 82

G

garbage 16, 20, 30, 57, 65, 89
Garrett vii, 45, 46
Garrett-Evangelical Theological Semi-
    nary vii, 45, 46
gender 50, 54, 73, 81, 82, 83, 87, 88,
    89
General Conference 9, 36, 55, 61, 62,
    66, 67, 74, 75, 76
Glen Home 47
God 1, 3, 4, 7, 10, 15, 21, 25, 28, 29,
    32, 35, 38, 42, 46, 57, 61, 62,
    64, 65, 76, 77, 85, 86, 87, 88,
    90, 91
Goodwill Industries 55
gospel 1, 2, 3, 4, 5, 6, 7, 9, 10, 11, 19,
    21, 26, 27, 31, 33, 34, 35, 36,
    37, 40, 41, 42, 43, 50, 56, 59,
    61, 63, 66, 79, 81, 86, 88

H

Halsted Street Institutional Church 10,
    25, 50
Helm, E. J. 55
Horton, Isabelle v, 1, 9, 10, 24, 25, 26,
    27, 31, 33, 36, 37, 38, 40, 41,
    45, 51, 65, 66, 68, 71, 73, 81,
    82, 89
hospital 39
House Committee on Un-American
    Activities 83
Huber, John Milton 58, 59, 64, 67
Hull House vii, 9, 10, 13, 26, 30, 31,
    37

I

immigrants 6, 8, 9, 10, 14, 30, 34, 39,
    60, 76, 87, 88
immigration 10, 33, 50, 60, 74

J

Jesus 6, 7, 8, 11, 15, 22, 28, 36, 38,
    42, 55, 60, 61, 63, 69, 80, 85,
    86, 88, 91
Judicial Council 80

K

King, William McGuire 6, 59

L

labor 2, 5, 14, 15, 18, 19, 22, 33, 39,
    56, 57, 58, 63, 64, 67, 74, 75,
    76, 77, 79, 87, 88, 89, 90
Loetze, Rudolph Hermann 6
love 1, 4, 7, 10, 21, 28, 32, 38, 62, 63,
    65, 68, 76, 86, 88, 90, 91

M

Condon, Maggie 17
materialism 32, 36, 43
McDowell, Mary v, 1, 9, 10, 13, 14,
    15, 17, 18, 19, 20, 21, 22, 23,
    33, 35, 41, 45, 54, 65, 66, 67,
    68, 71, 75, 78, 81, 82, 96
Mead, Margaret 90
Methodist Episcopal Church 6, 7, 8, 9,
    30, 40, 46, 53, 55, 56, 62, 63,
    64, 66, 67, 68, 72, 73, 74, 75,
    80, 81, 95
Methodist Federation for Social Action
    2, 55, 58, 59, 82, 90, 95
Methodist Federation for Social Service
    2, 7, 9, 10, 26, 41, 50, 54, 55,
    57, 58, 59, 61, 62, 67, 72, 74,
    79, 81, 85, 88, 94, 95, 96
Meyer, Josiah 25, 72
Meyer, Lucy Rider 8, 10, 25, 26, 33,
    72, 73, 79, 94

Willard, Frances 46, 79
Williams, Claude 74
Wilson, Woodrow 74
Woman's Foreign Missionary Society
        81
Woman's Home Missionary Society 7,
        8, 36, 45, 46, 47, 67, 81
World Court 68

Y

YWCA 74

Z

Zaring, Robb 53, 54